Praise for C

Schwartz-Chaney does a phenom complex, convoluted, and controversial concepts absolutely clear. Her passionate writing is simple and concise, allowing any reader to fully understand the enormity of the mutually inclusive connection between critical race theory and faith. *Critical Faith* is a must-read for believers and non-believers, as well as scholars and non-academics.

—Dr. Wendy M. Nicholson, PhD, executive director of diversity, equity, and inclusion, LaGuardia Community College

In her book *Critical Faith*, Dr. Joni Schwartz-Chaney casts a strong and focused light on an American appropriation of Christianity that has sadly accompanied, historically, the national acceptance of racism and colorism. Nevertheless, as a fervent Christian believer, she has written a text that is full of hope in what Christian congregations can be, even as she illuminates the tragic effects of our country's refusal largely to clearly see the effects of our past on the present. Explaining and using the lens of critical race theory to demystify the stories co-religionists tell one another about who American Christians are, Dr. Schwartz-Chaney successfully helps us to both understand and confront an enduring racial segregation in our pews. *Critical Faith* attempts to offer a rational way for millennial American Christians to comprehend ourselves, as the writing of Karl Barth aided a post-war Christianity and as James Cone gave clarity to Christians following the era of civil rights. Dr. Schwartz-Chaney successfully presents a way for Protestant and Catholic churches to be anti-racist and to see themselves as the prophet Micah suggested we are expected to be before our God.

—Rev. Gregory Chisholm, SJ, superior of the Jesuit community, Baltimore, Maryland; former pastor, St. Charles Borromeo Roman Catholic Church, Harlem, New York

In a time when segments of the Christian community have seemingly lost their minds—that is, the ability to think critically and biblically about issues of race—Dr. Schwartz-Chaney's book, *Critical Faith: What It Is, What It's Not, and Why It Matters*, is a breath of fresh air as she reclaims the issues of race and racism for the church today.

—Rev. Bob Smith, retired pastor, professor, and founding
director of the Fort Wayne School of Urban Ministry

Joni Schwartz-Chaney is a lifelong friend and a sister in Christ. I had the privilege of serving as her pastor during the formative years of her spiritual journey. I have always been impressed with her intellectual honesty and willingness to challenge conventional wisdom without resorting to self-righteous academic haughtiness. This book is a testament to her courage and tenacity while grappling with a controversial concept. I gladly recommend this important work, especially to the faith community where CRT has been largely and unfairly demonized. I would hope that the church in America would grant her a fair hearing and take her admonitions seriously.

—Rev. Seth G. Tidball, pastor, Lake Cumberland
Church of the Nazarene

CRITICAL FAITH

CRITICAL FAITH

What It Is, What It Isn't & Why It Matters

JONI SCHWARTZ-CHANEY

FORTRESS PRESS
MINNEAPOLIS

CRITICAL FAITH
What It Is, What It Isn't, and Why It Matters

Library of Congress Cataloging-in-Publication Data

Names: Schwartz, Joni, author.
Title: Critical faith : what it is, what it's not, and why it matters /
    Joni Schwartz-Chaney.
Description: Minneapolis : Fortress Press, [2024]
Identifiers: LCCN 2023045068 (print) | LCCN 2023045069 (ebook) | ISBN
    9781506491554 (print) | ISBN 9781506491561 (ebook)
Subjects: LCSH: Racism--Religious aspects--Christianity. | Critical race
    theory.
Classification: LCC BT734.2 .S334 2024 (print) | LCC BT734.2 (ebook) |
    DDC 277.308/3089--dc23/eng/20240116
LC record available at https://lccn.loc.gov/2023045068
LC ebook record available at https://lccn.loc.gov/2023045069

Cover designer: Brice Hemmer
Cover image: Stained, Emily Ridge Gallagher & R. B. Pollock, Jr. (Spoke and
Feather, LLC), © 2023

Print ISBN: 978-1-5064-9155-4
eBook ISBN: 978-1-5064-9156-1

To John R. Chaney

Contents

Contents

Preface

This book chose me. I am a follower of Christ, a church participant, an insider, and I felt a burden of obedience to write. To be sure, I have an uneasy relationship with organized religion while loving the community of believers—no doubt an imperfect and flawed follower but a follower just the same. An eclectic scholar, I am not a historian, social scientist, or legal expert, but as a researcher and teacher I have utilized critical race theory (CRT) for the past twenty years.

Recently I attended a megachurch that had a beloved white pastor, great worship, and an interracial congregation; I love the worship, the presence of the Holy Spirit, the people—I love the message of individual salvation through Jesus Christ. It is central to who I am. However, this individualized message is just one part of the gospel. This same power of transformation also speaks to history, cultures, current social contexts, and conflicts. It is to this collective salvation that this book speaks. My spiritual persuasion is Christianity, but I am not so naive as to think that God cannot be revealed through other traditions and revelations. God is God, after all.

As I write these words, I am scared and angry. Newscasters are reporting yet another public shooting, this time in Buffalo, New York, in a predominantly Black neighborhood at a Tops Friendly Market on a normal Saturday. Ten people are dead; three injured. Eleven victims were Black and two white, the result of a racially motivated hate crime. This time it is a teenage gunman espousing a white supremacist ideology inspired by replacement theory. His racist act is indicative of the dangers of misguided theory.

Theories matter. This book focuses on a very different theory: critical race theory, or CRT. *Critical Faith* is instructive of the power of smart theory to understand and heal. It is also instructive of one institution in America, the church, and its missed opportunity caused by dismissing and demonizing CRT. The Buffalo domestic terrorist attack evidences the endemic and persistent existence of racist thought in America. *Critical Faith* speaks to America's history and the Christian church's complicity—Protestant, evangelical, conservative, and Catholic—in that racist thought.

This writing is scary because, as I figure it, there are at least three strikes going against me. I am white writing about race. I am a woman writing about the church. And finally, I am an academic writing about God. As a white scholar, I may be targeted with charges of interest convergence and insensitivity to racial issues. As a white author, how can I presume to understand race and racism in America? Furthermore, my decades in evangelical churches make me wary that, as a woman, I will not be taken seriously.

My references to Christ, faith, spirituality, and Christianity will make some of my friends in the academy uncomfortable and perhaps dismissive. But as FDR is believed to have said, "Courage is not the absence of fear, but rather the assessment that something else is more important than fear." So I write this book because understanding CRT, race, and racism in the American church is crucial. I am willing to risk alienating people who are important to me. Writing is my act of protest, so I enter the fray. I have utilized CRT in my teaching of undergraduate and graduate students for twenty years. I view assaults on CRT as not only an attack on academic freedom, but also a missed opportunity for students to understand how race has shaped America's past and present. I see CRT as a tool to engage in conversations about racial identity and a framework to have overdue, intelligent, and civil discussions about race and its impact on all of us, whether we are aware of it or not. We do not live in a colorblind society. Race matters.

I experience Christ as a liberator: a liberator of my individual soul and a liberator at work in the kingdoms of this world. My lived experience of Christ is one of liberation: from my own sins in the traditional born-again sense; from sexist, oppressive systems within and without the church; and from the racist systems that have informed the history and contemporary culture of America in which I am complicit.

This book is an act of obedience to that Christ and to the church community. Critical faith matters.

Introduction

"Nothing in the world is more dangerous than sincere ignorance and conscientious stupidity."

—Martin Luther King Jr.

"Men despise religion, they hate it and are afraid it might be true. To cure that we have to begin by showing that religion is not contrary to reason."

—Blaise Pascal

Critical faith is a habit of intellectual labor and vitality. It is the union of reasoned argument and the truth of the spirit, the pursuit of reason and hunger for the mystical, individual spiritual conversion and responsible social engagement. Critical faith unifies the spirit, soul, and body. It welcomes research, science, and differences. It prizes spirited debate and a healthy dose of humility. Critical faith is the ability to hold ambiguity, balance doubt and belief, and to question yet commit. It is comfortable with paradox, accepts nuance, and connects the mind and body. It engages in civil discourse but rejects inauthenticity, intolerance, evil, and racism within the church. Critical faith loves the church and its people. It questions authority and stands with the poor and marginalized. It engages the whole person. Yet critical faith is hard to find.

Critical faith has not always been lost. High points in church history linked deep faith with the cultivation of the mind for God's glory.[1] Thomas Aquinas, Martin Luther, the Puritans and Quakers,

C. S. Lewis, Reinhold Niebuhr, Thomas Merton, Martin Luther King Jr., and Dietrich Bonhoeffer all exemplify critical faith. Major universities were originally faith-based: Harvard, Yale, and Dartmouth (Puritan); the College of William and Mary (Church of England); Princeton (Presbyterian); and Rutgers (Dutch Reformed Church) helped establish the church as an intellectual stronghold in early America.

The church in twenty-first-century America has devolved from its intellectual core. This loss is witnessed in the abandonment of scholarship, reasoned argument, science, and research, making way for a personalized, emotional, and sloppy theology. We have traded dialogue and listening for heated rhetoric and plugged ears. This change has taken some Christians down the road of conspiracy, confusion, and polarization. It leaves others ill-equipped to tackle the mammoth issues of the day, including racism.

WHAT DOES RACE HAVE TO DO WITH IT?

From the beginning, America has grappled with race. From 1619, when the first twenty enslaved Africans reached Virginia, to the ongoing displacement and murder of indigenous peoples, America has practiced domestic terrorism, and churches have too often been complicit. There was something rotten at the core of early American churches' embrace of slavery, a basic incoherence that has been called America's original sin.[2]

If we are honest, the pursuit of knowledge has not always led to truth even for those who professed faith. Knowledge alone will not secure racial justice. Our best hope is a critical faith—anchored to the courage of the spirit of Christ—that drives radical and revolutionary love. It will require the individual witness of organic intellectuals driven by their commitment to Christ. But it will take more than individual witness. Moving beyond racism in America will demand critical faith of the church collective.

CRITICAL FAITH AND CRITICAL RACE THEORY

If it is true that the church has lost the ability to think critically, particularly in regard to its original sin of racism, then tools to understand this ongoing crisis are required. Critical race theory is one such tool. However, CRT is rejected in many church circles as Marxist, of the devil, divisive, and anti-God—a scapegoat for all things race. This is a mistake at best and slander at worst.

Critical Faith opens by defining CRT and explaining why it is polarizing. It goes on to examine the life of Derrick Bell, a major CRT founder, and the tenets of the theory. Topics include the history of race and racism, the difference between individual and institutionalized racism, wokeism, intersectionality, counter-storytelling, Black Lives Matter, white allies, the Bible, and CRT. These tenets are used to analyze white and interracial Christian churches in America in their institutional manifestations: Protestant (both fundamentalist and modernist), Catholic, evangelical, conservative of all varieties, and independent. Black churches are also engaged in this discussion as it relates to Black theology.

CRT points to the permanence of race as it is institutionalized in the church. CRT makes certain things visible that may not ordinarily be evident, especially to white people. This book challenges us to understand the world in which we live through serious analysis, combining rationality with humility and social action. It maintains that this is Christ's call to us. The hope is that the ensuing pages will show that "religion is not contrary to reason,"[3] and that as critical faith utilizes the tool of CRT, we might see both the Church and race through new eyes.

NOTES

1 Noll, *Scandal of the Evangelical Mind*.
2 Wallis, *America's Original Sin*.
3 Pascal, *Pensées*.

CHAPTER ONE

Critical Race Theory

A Brief Introduction

"The mind governed by the flesh is death, but the mind governed by the Spirit is life and peace."

—Romans 8:6 NIV

On May 14, 2022, Buffalo, New York, was the site of a mass shooting. Thirteen people were shot; eleven were Black and two were white. Ten were killed. The perpetrator was a white eighteen-year-old who wrote a 180-page hate-filled manifesto that referenced the great replacement theory. On August 11, 2017, white supremacist groups, including the KKK, gathered in Charlottesville, Virginia, for a violent two-day rally during which a counterprotester was killed. The great replacement theory was referenced there, too. On October 27, 2018, an attack on a Jewish synagogue in Pittsburgh, Pennsylvania, killed eleven. The shooter espoused the great replacement theory. On August 3, 2019, twenty-three people died in El Paso, Texas, when Latino shoppers were targeted by a terrorist who left behind a document referencing the great replacement theory. While the violence itself dominated the headlines, the ideology underwriting these acts of violence was alarmingly consistent.

Replacement theory is a far-right conspiracy that asserts that people of color are "being brought into the United States and other Western countries to replace white voters to achieve a political agenda."[1] It is often touted by anti-immigration groups and white supremacists. The fear is that white people are being replaced by people of color, a fear that motivates these theorists to use violence to preserve the white race. The theory, rooted in early 1900's French nationalism, is contemporaneously espoused by Renaud Camus, a French writer who popularized the idea in his 2011 book *Le grand replacement*.[2] But it is pseudoscience. It lacks any support from systematic observation, qualitative research, or quantitative research.[3] Some scholars disdain even calling replacement theory a "theory" because it is not substantiated through testing, not compatible with evidence, not peer-reviewed, and does not use the scientific method.[4] Bluntly, it is "theory" based on distortion and outright lies.

THEORY MATTERS

Theory frames the way we understand our world and how we act in response. Unlike replacement theory, most theories are based on the scientific method with rigorous and systematic observations that are repeatedly tested and often expanded to integrate well-founded and substantiated claims. Theories are reasoned explanations of natural phenomena that result from careful data collection and analysis over time. Effective theories frame our thinking. For scientists, these evidenced, peer-reviewed, well-substantiated explanations of the natural world or human behavior can incorporate laws, hypotheses, tenets, and facts. For example, gravitational theory explains how fruit falls from trees and why astronauts float in space.

Theories explain both individuals and groups. For example, *social penetration theory*, a well-established theory in the field of communication, states that as interpersonal relationships evolve, communication patterns between two individuals move from superficial exchanges to intimate ones. Applied *social penetration theory* supports decision-making around the quality and authenticity of human relationships and guides decisions affecting marriage, divorce, personal boundaries, and healthy friendships. *Systems theory,* of which there are multiple types from distinct scientific disciplines (biology, social science, organizational communication, etc.), analyzes how cells in the body, groups of people in a society, or parts of an organization interrelate as a whole. *Systems theory* helps us evaluate our organizations—like churches, families, and workplaces—and can direct us toward change.

Theories are the foundation of most academic disciplines. There are social science, biological, psychological, education, physics, spiritual, and legal studies theories. They are often questioned, tested, disputed, and sometimes abandoned. Besides explaining facts, theories allow scientists to make predictions about future behavior and phenomena. As theories are tested over time, new evidence supports or contradicts them. This allows theories to be refined or rejected. As long as key tenets of a theory prove accurate and hold through ongoing testing, observation, and ability to explain the world, then a theory is considered strong,

THE CHURCH AND THEORY

Science and the church have had a long, divisive relationship. This age-old dynamic was evident most recently during the Covid-19 pandemic, where elements of the church rejected the advice of scientists from the Centers for Disease Control and Prevention (CDC) and the National Institutes of Health (NIH). This uneasy relationship has deep historical roots. Since 1633, when Galileo faced the Roman Catholic Inquisition for his discovery that the earth revolves around the sun, parts of the church have been skeptical of science.[5] Ancient societies and the early Christian church believed that the earth is the center of the universe because God valued man. Man was made in God's image; therefore, man's habitation must be the center of God's creation. The intricate, complex epicycles of the Ptolemaic model of the solar system gave the geocentric worldview predictive power. Galileo disproved this theory and instead espoused heliocentrism, the astronomical theory that the earth and all other planetary bodies orbited around the sun. When he published his theory, Galileo was accused of heresy and taken to trial by the church, remaining in house arrest upon his conviction. Additionally, those church members who espoused heliocentric theory were excommunicated. Not until 1993 did the pope formally acquit Galileo of heresy.[6]

More recent schisms between science and religion include evolutionary theory. In her book *Faith Unraveled*, Rachel Held Evans tells the story of growing up in Dayton, Tennessee, the location of the Scopes Monkey Trial of 1925, where the rift between evolutionary and creationist theory took center stage. John Scopes, a high school science teacher, stood trial for teaching evolutionary theory. Clarence Darrow, a famous lawyer and proponent of Darwinism, represented Scopes, and William Jennings Bryan, a populist politician and anti-evolutionist, was the prosecutor. The trial pitted the modernist view that evolution is not inconsistent with religion against fundamentalist perspectives that hold a literal reading of the Bible. The debates were broadcast on radio for the nation to hear. Christians across the country supported Bryan. The case ended with Scopes found guilty, but Darrow arguing convincingly and winning over the public in favor of evolutionary theory.

Contemporary Catholics and most mainline Protestants accept evolutionary theory. In the words of Francis Collins, Christian and renowned genetic scientist:

> Evolution has been very much on the scene for 150 years, and the science that supports Darwin's theory has gotten stronger and stronger over those decades. That evidence is particularly strong today given the ability to study DNA and to see the way in which it undergirds Darwin's theory in a marvelously digital fashion.[7]

Collins, former director of the National Human Genome Research Institute and the NIH, professes faith and practices science without contradiction.[8] Today many scientists and moderate Christians would agree that both science and religion have a role to play in understanding the modern world. Church and scientific theories need not be pitted against one another; no controversy needs to exist. By their very nature, theories are challenged, questioned, and tested by scientists. But sometimes this challenging comes not from theorists, but from clerics (as was the case with heliocentric, evolutionary, stem cell, and climate change theories).

CRITICAL RACE THEORY UNDER ATTACK

CRT is the latest theoretical idea challenged by the church. In some ways, the opposition appears more like an attack than a challenge. CRT is a rational explanation for the prevalence of racism in America as manifested in law since the 1960's civil rights movement. Like other scientific theories, CRT frames our understanding and can guide our actions. In this case, the understanding is about racism in America. A relatively new theory, developed in the 1970s and '80s, CRT recognizes both that there is no Black/white racial binary in nature and that racism impacts people of color in diverse ways, thus explaining the creation of LatCrit, TribalCrit, and AsianCRT. These corollary theories explore the intersection of race, ethnicity, and colorism, and speak to the robust breadth of CRT.

In the 1970s and early '80s, Harvard law professor Derrick Bell's philosophical writings formed the foundation of what would become CRT. Bell was the first Black professor to teach at Harvard Law School. In the early days of CRT, Bell, along with other legal scholars like Alan Freeman, Richard Delgado, and Kimberlé Crenshaw, saw that the laws passed during the civil rights movement didn't result in real change, and they wanted to understand why.[9]

From the first 1989 workshop, held in a religious convent in Madison, Wisconsin, much of the thinking behind CRT came from critical legal studies and radical feminism. A major premise of critical legal theory is that the law is intertwined with social issues, informed by historical and social contexts, and has inherent social biases. Radical

5

feminism proposes that women's experiences are affected by social dynamics such as class, race, and sexual orientation, and that male supremacy needs elimination. After rigorous debate, which is ongoing, CRT's main tenets and themes include the following:

- Racism is ordinary, not aberrational.
- Systems of white supremacy serve to the advantage of whites and are often colorblind, so are hard to detect.
- Legal progress (and setbacks) for people of color generally benefit white people.
- Race is socially constructed, not biologically or scientifically valid.
- Humans are complex with overlapping identities, ethnicities, and allegiances (intersectionality and anti-essentialism).
- History has been told primarily by those in power; therefore, the counternarratives of the oppressed must be voiced.

CRT critiques liberal legal frameworks that espouse colorblindness of constitutional law regarding race because the law is not neutral. It is informed by social and political context. Colorblind theories of jurisprudence can thus hide ways in which they privilege one group of people over another. CRT acknowledges that the law can be complicit in sustaining an unjust social order, especially as it pertains to race. CRT legal theorists maintain that while the law can be used to deepen racial inequality, it also has the potential to move toward racial equality and social justice.[10] Kimberlé Crenshaw, a legal scholar at UCLA and Columbia, coined the term *critical race theory*. The name denotes an analytic and reflective bent that is *evaluative* in its research orientation of systems of power and *activist* in its orientation to transforming those systems. CRT is a theory aimed at producing social change as it relates to race in America.[11] This is CRT in brief. The remainder of this book further defines and analyzes each CRT tenet, especially as they relate to the church in America.

WHAT CRT IS NOT

The recent anti-CRT bills in Congress and the attacks on CRT in workplace diversity training are the latest iteration of a hundred-year-old movement to control American identity, suppress racial dialogue, and neutralize the historical narrative around race. Schools and workplaces have long been battlegrounds of ideological wars. Unfortunately, the conservative Christian church and some of its leaders have joined in. Some are spreading the message that CRT is inconsistent with Christianity and something to be feared.[12] This "something" has been labeled a worldview, an ideology, a cult, a conspiracy, a political perspective, and even a religion. CRT is none of these.[13] Neither this new round of resistance to CRT nor its arguments are fresh.

First, CRT is not a worldview. It is a theory developed by American legal scholars in response to the lack of policy implementation and legislative changes after the civil rights movement. Its core scholars are a multiracial group of Americans. In addition to Bell, Delgado, Freeman, and Crenshaw, notable scholars include Cheryl Harris, Charles R. Lawrence III, Mari Matsuda, and Patricia Williams. This theory, widely appealing as an analytic tool, is used in other parts of the world to look at race. However, it was developed to address an American context and how race operates in this country and its laws. It is not global. It is not a "theory of everything." It is conscious of its range of applicability and rigorously controls its use only to those sets of data to which it applies.

In that same vein, CRT is not an ideology, creed, or doctrine. CRT does not espouse any political or prescriptive economic framework—whether democratic, democratic socialism, liberalism, libertarianism, conservatism, totalitarianism, progressivism, capitalism, or Marxism. It critiques elements of neoliberalism, but doing so hardly makes it Marxist. There are individuals who believe US capitalism supports classism and racism, that slavery propelled capitalism and economic gain in the service of white supremacy, and that capitalism has created a class of economic elite. Some Christians hold these views.[14] But CRT as a theory is not anti-capitalist, nor is it Marxist or anti-democratic. (More will be discussed about this in Chapter 2.)

CRT is not a theology. It does not study the nature of God. Nor is it a religion that espouses doctrines, follows a sacred text, or prescribes belief in and worship of a higher power. It does not ask the big questions, like: *Is there a God? How do we determine right from wrong? What happens after I die?* CRT scholars, writings, and tenets do not approach anything like theology or religion.

Nor is CRT a cult. Cults are sects of relatively small groups of people with strong unexamined and addictive devotion to a charismatic leader. CRT features no insular community bound by adherence to the teachings of a leader. CRT has no leader. Not even Derrick Bell was ever its sole spokesperson. Other leading scholars—like Mari Matsuda, Kimberlé Crenshaw, Richard Delgado, and Daniel Solorzano—teach in various universities, participate in think tanks across the country, and interpret the theory through diverse academic disciplines. Interactions are collaborative, inclusionary, and anything but insular. During the theory's initial development, there was intense disagreement, difference of opinion, rigorous critique of one another's scholarship, and self-examination based on peer review challenges. This is nothing like a cult, where divergent views are suppressed and dissent is prohibited. On the contrary, CRT has always welcomed debate and intellectual challenges.

Nor is CRT a conspiracy or propaganda by Black people, Marxists, CRT scholars, or atheists. In fact, it is a diverse and divergent group primarily consisting of legal experts, scholars, historians, social scientists, educators, and people of faith who have worked for decades to understand and change the dynamics of racism in America. Proponents of CRT are not part of a shadow government plotting revolution. They aren't bent on indoctrinating school children. Such brainwashing is antithetical to CRT and to the scientific method that it employs. Nowhere in its writings or scholarship does CRT promote scheming against white people or plotting to overthrow capitalism.[15]

MAKING CRT A CATCHPHRASE

The recent attack on CRT began with a September 4, 2020, memo directed by former president Trump to the heads of executive departments and agencies of the US government. A portion is quoted here:

> The President has directed me [R. Vought Director Budget & Management] to ensure that Federal agencies cease and desist from using taxpayer dollars to fund these divisive, un-American propaganda training sessions. . . . All agencies are directed to begin to identify all contracts or other agency spending related to any training on "critical race theory," "white privilege," or any other training or propaganda effort that teaches or suggests either (1) that the United States is an inherently racist or evil country or (2) that any race or ethnicity is inherently racist or evil. In addition, all agencies should begin to identify all available avenues within the law to cancel any such contracts and/or to divert Federal dollars away from these un-American propaganda training sessions.[16]

Several things are clear from this memo: CRT is used to represent all anti-racist efforts, is labeled as un-American propaganda, and is mischaracterized in both its intent and content. It targets CRT as un-American, but CRT is pro-American in its truth-telling and inclusive accounts of American history. It encourages dialogue to better understand the role and impact of race in this country. This is democratic in every sense of the word. The aim of CRT scholars has always been to make America truer to its democratic principles by studying its systems, history, and social constructs. As it critiques white privilege and white supremacy, it does so in the service of a more democratic society.

President Biden rescinded Trump's executive order when he first entered the office of the presidency. By then, though, the damage had been done. Unfortunately, some Christians and churches were among those who accepted the claims about CRT uncritically. And to this day it appears that some Christians are, at best, confused about the matter. This confusion has fed existing fears and accelerated polarization. As one friend and scholar said to me, we need a "CRT for Dummies" to clear up all the misinformation. Chapter 2 discusses polarization, tribalism, and the making of CRT to be the enemy in American society and within the Christian church.

Broadening the scope of CRT to encompass almost any concept of race has led to at least thirty-six states and local municipalities introducing legislation that could ban its teaching in schools and the workplace. The term has been co-opted by those opposed to talking about racism, those against reexamining and truthfully telling American history in its totality, and those opposed to diversity training and race education in our schools. This repression is an attack on free speech, and the confusion and demonization of CRT that contributes to it has left an unhealthy vacuum in understanding that conspiratorial thinking is all too willing to fill.

FILLING THE VACUUM

James Baldwin observed that "The people who settled [America] had a fatal flaw."[17] They knew that Native Americans, Mexicans, and African slaves were human beings, but because the settlers were predominantly Christians, they had to rationalize their views—deciding these "others" were not human, but chattel—so that they could justify their exploitation and slaveholding before God.[18] This was the original "big lie."

When we do not have an adequate theory to comprehend our history, our country's relationship with race, and the continued imprint of race on today's churches and societies, conspiracy theories fill the void. Remnants of the big lie—that the racial caste system is natural, metaphysical, or even willed by God—resurface in the replacement theory espoused by white nationalists. The results can turn violent. In June 2015, a young white terrorist in Charleston, South Carolina, murdered nine Black church members. Like the terrorist in Buffalo, he drew upon replacement theory to explain racial dynamics and to lash out in hate. This killer was a baptized member of the Lutheran church. In his book *Dear Church*, Lutheran pastor Lenny Duncan calls out the church for failing to hold the killer accountable for his white supremacist theories.[19] Yet, if churches themselves lack the tools to understand race and its history, they will be unable to offer their members an account of that history to displace the conspiracies. Not many people deny that racism exists, but defining how it works in American life is complicated. Many fail to understand how it came to be, why it impacts us so much, and why it seems so hard to eradicate. The result is avoidance, confusion, and defensiveness.

Therefore, theory is crucial. It fills the vacuum of ignorance and displaces misinformation. CRT is a good theory for making sense of racism's persistence and tenacity. It is also an effective tool for understanding the American church's relationship to race historically and contemporaneously, as well as the potential and power of the gospel to dismantle systems of oppression, whether they are the product of our own personal sin or the sins of a nation. After all, isn't this the call of the cross?

NOTES

1 National Immigration Forum, "'Great Replacement' Theory."
2 National Immigration Forum.
3 Ekman, "Great Replacement."
4 Gottlieb, "Not a Theory."
5 Suran, "Separation of Church and Science."
6 Held Evans, *Faith Unraveled*.
7 Pew Research Center, "Evidence for Belief."
8 Collins, *Language of God*.
9 Delgado and Stefancic, *Critical Race Theory*.
10 George, "A Lesson."
11 Delgado and Stefancic.
12 Lee, "Critical Race Theory."
13 Strachan, *Christianity and Wokeness*; Dodson, *Critical Race Theory*; Lesperance, *Critical Race Theory*.

14 Duncan, *Dear Church.*
15 Gonzalez and Butcher, "Purging Whiteness."
16 Vought, "Training."
17 Baldwin, *Cross of Redemption.*
18 Baldwin.
19 Duncan, *Dear Church.*

CHAPTER TWO

Polarization, Tribalism, and Making CRT the Enemy

"Get away from any man who always argues every time he talks."
—The Desert Fathers LXIV

I spent much of my adult life worshipping with congregants from one of the most loving Christian churches in America—the Brooklyn Tabernacle. At one time, it was known for its Grammy Award–winning choir and worship, but it was dear to me for the love of Christ its members showed. I have since left the church, but it is clear after speaking with remaining members that something changed during the 2016 presidential campaign season. Longtime friends and church members engaged in heated and accusatory rhetoric, online and in person, fracturing relationships and straining previously loving communities. Polarization and tribalism entered the church pews.

Like America as a whole, church members divided into opposite groupings along the lines of conservative and liberal. Opinions were no longer nuanced but concentrated in opposing extremes impervious to reasoned argument—binary thinking. Civil discourse was rare, replaced by volatile name-calling and emotional tirades fueled not just by partisanship, but by negative partisanship, and therefore a belief not in the rightness of one's position, but in the danger inherent in the other side's. Sadly, the discourse was mixed with spiritual assaults and judgment. People on both sides accused others of being non-Christians, stupid Christians, or deceived.

One of the most public of these breaches involved Russell Moore, an eminent Southern Baptist leader who denounced Trump at a church convention that embraced the former president. Moore was ostracized, severely criticized, and experienced threats to his family.[1] Moore was not alone; church tribalism prevailed across the country, with congregants demonizing one another. Within this climate of contention, CRT was a frequent target of attack.

MAKING CRT AN ENEMY

The September 4, 2020 memo directed by former president Trump brought CRT to public awareness but distorted it to encompass all things racial. Before, most Americans had never heard of CRT. Once they had, it became a household word connoting anti-Americanism, communism, and hatred of white people. In the spirit of McCarthyism, politicians and church leaders pounced on CRT with vociferous rants in pulpits, community centers, schoolboards, social media, and publications.[2]

As of early 2022, thirty-six states had either introduced or adopted policies restricting the teaching of race and racism, using CRT as a catchall term.[3] Anti-CRT publications have flourished, with many like Voddie Baucham's *Fault Lines* catastrophizing the fall of Christianity in America. Diana Lesperance's *Critical Race Theory: An Introduction from a Biblical Historical Perspective* connected CRT to the anti-war movement, the Black Power movement (which she separates from the civil rights movement), the feminist movement, and liberation theology. Lesperance prophesied that if Southern Baptists and other churches embrace CRT, the Bible will then be compromised, causing "division, civil war, and human suffering."[4] These ongoing "sky is falling" proclamations were common on social media, in schoolboard meetings, and in print. One writer went so far as to title his booklet *Critical Race Theory: A Doctrine of Devils That Is Captivating the Minds of Americans*.[5] There is no question that in some church circles, CRT is the enemy, if not the anti-Christ.

ARGUMENTS USED AGAINST CRT ARE NOT NEW

The current arguments against CRT are eerily familiar. They've been used repeatedly in past decades.[6] CRT, it is charged, is "liberal." Evolved from Marxist communist roots, it fosters a victim mentality within Black people, teaches hatred of white people, is opposed to the Gospel, rewrites American history, and, when taught to white children, will make them feel guilty and ashamed. In extreme instances, attacks go beyond the theory to targeting CRT proponents themselves as troublemakers and revolutionaries. Advocates and adherents are those who have turned away from God, liars against whom the judgment of God will strike.[7]

Calling someone or some idea socialist and tying them to communism has been a reliable rhetorical weapon since before the Cold War and McCarthyism. Sometimes the name-calling varies: cultural Marxists, socialist democrats, postmodern neo-Marxists, communist democrats, and postmodernists. To be called these terms is to be the boogeyman. Dr. Martin Luther King Jr. is now revered, but was once slandered as a communist, smeared as a con man, reviled as a liar, and cast as a threat to America.[8] The late Pat Robertson, media mogul and religious broadcaster, called CRT a "monstrous evil." Trump called it "toxic propaganda threatening to destroy America." This kind of name-calling is not limited solely to American church leaders and politicians. In Britain and Australia, CRT is a so-called illegal concept that is thought to lead to a "segregated society reducing citizens to their racial essence."[9]

Christian writers and speakers also deride their opponents using religious terms that have existing negative connotations among conversative churches, such as *social gospel, Protestant liberalism,* and *Black liberation theology.* Labeling may seem harmless, but can result in stereotypes when used without definitions or justification. Such labeling often puts people and ideas into binary categories: good/bad, right wing/left wing, for/against, moral/immoral. This dichotomizing gives us a simplistic view of the world that cannot accurately reflect reality.

Both Robertson and Carol Swain, a university professor who travels the conservative and Christian media junket, repeatedly use superlatives, exaggeration, and loaded language: "every corner of America," "dangerous weaponization," "poisoning our children," white oppressors and non-white victims, and CRT will "destroy our country." These are words of war. Swain goes on to say the theory is based on "division and has no place in the church."[10] When Florida governor Ron DeSantis signed a controversial bill banning CRT in Florida, he called CRT "indoctrination" that "[teaches] children to hate each other and hate their country."[11] Voddie Baucham, a prominent Southern Baptist leader and writer, said that CRT has "its own saints and own laws" and is a "looming catastrophe" for the church.[12] This rhetoric would be laughable if its ad nauseam approach did not breed fear and ignorance. Taken to an extreme, polarizing rhetoric fuels the directly harmful practices of dictatorships and demagogues, moving beyond words to physical violence.

CRT's sensational critics also trade in the tired trope that CRT fosters a victim mentality in Black people. This smear tactic is reminiscent of other weaponized terms like *super predator* (for Black youth), *welfare queen, single-parent families,* and *the urban poor*—all code words for Black dependency. Any social program that seeks to ameliorate historic social exclusion through government policy (e.g., affirmative action, Pell grants) is portrayed as unfairly supporting certain groups, creating dependency, and disadvantaging white people. Some of today's terms may be new, but the underlying logic is not.

Another new version on an old argument is that policy and social norms supporting racial equity for children of color will harm white children. We now know, for instance, that the busing policies of the 1960s and 1970s, put in place to promote desegregation, improved outcomes for Black children and did no harm to white children.[13] However, like then, the historical outcry was about the improvement in social outcomes for Black people coming at the expense of white people. Today's line of protest maintains that white children will be made to feel guilt and shame if they are taught about race, racism, and diversity.

In an ironic twist, today's critics of CRT's emphasis on the history of race, society, and law claim that history will be rewritten. Rather than teach history, they seek to ban it. Autocrats have long understood that directing the historical narrative is an essential element of control. What people believe about their own history informs how they view the present. In a democracy, multiple viewpoints exist alongside multiple histories of experience. They push and pull one another so as to curtail false narratives. Hearing the whole history—the good, the bad, and the ugly—is crucial for a functional democracy. Unfortunately, much of the teaching of American history has ignored key inflection points in the story of race, including Native American genocide, slavery, Japanese internment, lynching, Jim Crow, and the Tulsa Massacre. This selective storytelling is not just an aversion to difficult topics. Even key events in the slow realization of justice, such as the promulgation of the end of slavery being commemorated with the Juneteenth holiday, have only recently entered the consciousness of white Americans.

These unoriginal, untrue arguments are percolating in American churches.[14] Misinformation about the supposed spiritual dangers of CRT is making the situation even more insidious. CRT is branded as both un-American and anti-Gospel. Furthermore, the tone of the dialogue among Christians makes active listening and critical thinking rare. Toxic condemnations abound.

The Southern Baptist Convention (SBC) is the nation's largest Protestant denomination, and for the last two years, it has been divided over CRT, white privilege, and "woke" culture, along with the perennially contested issue of women in leadership and the institutional response to sexual abuse within Southern Baptist Convention churches.[15] These issues are the same ones that are brewing in the evangelical movement and the Catholic Church. The Conservative Baptist Network (CBN), a large splinter group of SBC, has made it clear that debates over CRT in the church will not soon subside. In an address to conservative supporters after failing to pass a CRT ban in a resolution, CBN leader Rod Martin dramatically proclaimed: "We will come back next year. And the next and the next. . . . All the apostles but one went to a martyr's death. . . . We will not stop; we are here to the death!" These words sound like a war cry, rallying church members through calls to a manufactured martyrdom. The remainder of this chapter deconstructs each of the myths these anti-CRT voices routinely express, with the goal of explaining how embracing CRT is an opportunity for the church.

MYTH #1: CRT HAS MARXIST ROOTS

Neither CRT nor critical legal studies (CLS), from which CRT was born, was developed by Marxists. They did not originate in some totalitarian system. Nor does CRT have its roots in communism, where resources and property are owned by the state for distribution to the people, or socialism, where all citizens of a country own an equal share of the economic resources. The founders of CRT were firmly in alliance with democracy. They understood modern social theory that drew in part from Marx; however, this does not make them socialists, communists, or Marxists. Anyone who accuses CRT or CLS scholars of being ideologically totalitarian or Marxist is spreading fallacies.[16]

CLS was developed in and largely limited to the United States. The legal scholars who crafted it were influenced by European philosophers, including Karl Marx, Max Weber, Max Horkheimer, Antonio Gramsci, and Michel Foucault. But they also drew from the school of legal realism of the 1920s and '30s. Legal realism theory proposes that laws come from social interests and public policy. When deciding cases, then, judges must consider those interests and policies, not only abstract rules. Context of the law was important, not just the letter of the law. CRT brought these insights to the question of colorblind application of the law, which in social context was anything but colorblind.

In one sense, CLS and CRT can be legitimately said to draw from Marxist thought insofar as they critique capitalist society, analyze oppressed/oppressor relationships, and strive against inequity. But one need not be a Marxist to make these critiques, and one does not need Marx to make them. The Bible contains many of these same connections and themes. As Christian apologist Mark Legg notes, some CRT theorists are religious as well as patriotic:

> CRT is . . . not Marxist in key ways. CRT adherents almost never advocate for the abolition of property, and they focus on social issues, not just economic ones. Some draw from CRT simply to critique how American society can be built better and with great equality for people across racial lines. They study history, sociology, and politics to work for a better solution. Many CRT advocates are religious, whereas Marxism says religion is "the opium of the masses." Many CRT proponents consider themselves patriots, like Crenshaw.[17]

As Legg points out, CRT is broad in its interdisciplinary focus and is not opposed to religion. Its primary focus is racial progress within the confines of democracy. That interdisciplinary focus extends well beyond European critical philosophy. Crenshaw explains that the philosophical roots of CRT also draw from the work of Frederick Douglass, Sojourner Truth, W. E. B. Du Bois, Frantz Fanon, and Martin Luther King Jr.—a diverse group of intellectuals and activists with divergent political and religious affiliations. CRT's formation was a critique of and response to the legal system that had developed after the civil rights movement. Its goal was to understand why racial progress had been stymied despite ostensible gains in legal recognition and protection.[18] CRT is an activist theory with roots deep in democracy. And although it is a response to the shortcomings of the civil rights movement, it also advances that very tradition.

While Marxism focuses on material wealth and power in capitalist societies, CRT focuses on institutionalized racism within American democracy and its legal, educational, healthcare, criminal justice, financial, and housing systems.

MYTH #2: CRT TEACHES VICTIMHOOD

Opponents of CRT argue that the theory makes Black people see themselves as victims by shifting responsibility for one's circumstances from the individual to institutions. These same opponents view CRT's message as the opposite of the "pulling yourself up by the bootstraps" philosophy and its celebration of personal responsibility. The idea of "pulling yourself up by the bootstraps," and the rugged individualism it reflects, has been ingrained in American mythology since the nineteenth century, but it originally meant then the opposite of what it does today. Ironically, it once meant trying to do something that was impossible (you cannot lift your body up by merely your shoestrings).[19] Today, though, it expresses opposition to social programs (affirmative action, the Affordable Care Act, Pell grants, etc.) that seek to provide healthcare and educational, employment, and housing opportunities to disadvantaged groups. Opponents of CRT insist that these programs breed dependency and victimhood.

This argument, though, is fallacious. Evidence shows that places with robust social welfare programs, including Canada and Europe, have higher labor market participation than the US for working-age adults. The existence of a social safety net does not incentivize dependency or make victims out of citizens. Furthermore, the myth of self-reliance assumes that white Americans achieved social mobility by their own efforts. But the Homestead Acts, Land-grant universities, New Deal programs, and G.I. Bill (to name but a few) were all social programs meant to benefit white people. CRT critics often invoke their own biographies and triumphs over adversity as evidence that initiative and personal responsibility are all that are required to succeed. But life is never that simple. Some of us can run the triathlon and some of us cannot, no matter how hard we might train.[20]

Critics of CRT will sometimes concede that a university or law school classroom is an acceptable venue for these conversations. But these same critics maintain that they are not appropriate for K–12 classes. Of course, CRT is not being taught or discussed in K–12 classrooms. It is taught only in universities, predominantly in law schools. Where it is taught, CRT is a prism to understand how racism in America operates within institutions and systems. As such, it does not negate personal responsibility, individual choice, hard work, integrity, or individual agency. Whether or not one inherits social advantages (inherited wealth, class, race, educational access, etc.) does not imply that one doesn't want to work, doesn't want to contribute, or doesn't take pride in living up to one's full potential. CRT never states that the notions of merit and excellence are racist, or that individuals shouldn't strive to achieve their best. In fact, Derrick Bell, the father of CRT, wrote about faith, courage, effort, self-reliance, persistence, and integrity as key values in his book *Ethical Ambition*.[21]

CRT is not a theory of individual success or failure. It is a broad lens through which we can study the role of race in America beyond individual success or failure. CRT examines spheres of living that embrace the individual but have their primary meaning in the social: housing, employment, healthcare, segregation, education, criminal justice, and the church. CRT promotes awareness of structures and policies where racism becomes socially and systemically entrenched. But it teaches resistance, not victimhood.[22]

By positioning racism outside of individual acts and within institutional frameworks, CRT spurs determination to personal work for progress in one's own life and in the lives of our collective. The activism that it inspires is itself addressed to those very institutions. It is why so much of today's activism concerns systemic policy issues instead of individual grievances: police reform policy, voting rights legislation, prison reform, and healthcare activism. Rather than victimization, CRT is a hopeful activist theory that promotes resilience in the face of institutional harms and courage to democratically affect changes to those institutions.

After encountering CRT decades ago during my doctoral studies, I felt less helpless, less inept in talking about racial progress, and more empowered to work with people of color to combat racism. The myth of Black self-victimization is a smokescreen for those unwilling to face the real problems of racism in America inherent in our institutions and policies.

MYTH #3: CRT HARMS WHITE CHILDREN

According to Alabama legislator Chris Pringle, "[CRT] basically teaches that certain children are inherently bad people because of the color of their skin." While such political talking points hardly merit a response, this trope has become increasingly common and so requires a rebuttal. CRT does not teach hate of anyone. It does not teach that white people are inherently racist and privileged. The theory does not assert that people be primarily viewed as members of a racial group rather than as individuals. The purpose of the theory is not shame and guilt, but racial understanding and systemic change.[23]

Blaming and fault-finding are not productive. But defining race, promoting knowledge of racial history, challenging systems of power that are unfair, tackling the complexities of discrimination and prejudice, listening to people with divergent life experiences, grappling with the possibility that our thinking is skewed, and owning up to truths about the role of race in America have tremendous value. Unless we teach about race in our schools (which does not necessarily mean teaching CRT), we won't move forward.

At age-appropriate stages, CRT skillfully teaches a way of viewing race that transfers focus from individual acts of racism to racism in policies, programs, and institutions. This analysis is a tool that can help white people to see racism operating within a society beyond themselves and their own virtues or vices. This vantage point can be liberating in assisting white people to comprehend why the US is not a colorblind society, in providing objectivity when talking about race beyond white fragility, and in choosing to embrace the anti-racist work that we all need to do. "We need to be very clear," notes anti-racist scholar Tim Wise, "critical race theory is not only legitimate, it is absolutely valuable and critical if we're going to solve the problems that confront us."[24]

My twelve-year-old granddaughter's favorite school subject is history. Ella is white and lives in Texas. Texas House Bill 3979, commonly called Texas's critical race theory law, discourages and limits learning about racism, sexism, and their relation to American history. It was passed on July 16, 2021. This law will leave Ella and other Texas children with a decidedly narrow view of history and the impact of race. It will, in short, make her education deficient. Included in Texas Bill 3979 is the prohibition of teaching the 1619 Project, which centers the Black experience of slavery in the formation of this country. Shameful. I know what book I'll be giving Ella for Christmas.

MYTH #4: CRT IS REWRITING HISTORY

I attended what were considered good schools growing up, but now know that I was taught a redacted version of American history. The obscured portions were many: Native American genocide, Reconstruction, Jim Crow, and events like Tulsa's Black Wall Street, the La Placita raid, and numerous acts of domestic terrorism—all related to race and ethnicity. How is it possible that one can graduate from high school and never study in any depth such pivotal historic events? Our textbooks never covered these topics, and our teachers never taught them. We received a whitewashed version of American history.

CRT supports the perspective that we need to hear the voices of people of color in the telling of American history. Who tells that history and from whose positionality it is told matters. It is like the Zimbabwean proverb: "Until the lions have their own historians, the history of the hunt will always glorify the hunter." CRT encourages telling history from multiple viewpoints in order to grasp as complete a history as possible.

In a democracy, this multiplicity should be welcomed. We need multiple perspectives, many historians, and we need the whole story. This is not a rewriting of history; instead, it is research that provides accuracy, complexity, and transparency. It has been called revisionist, but CRT uses the term *counter-storytelling*. Most American history is written from the perspective of white men of European descent, the dominant narrative. Including the perspectives of the marginalized provides a more complete history. Historical narratives of both good and bad events should be told and taught. In doing so, our American heroes may become less pristine, and America may not seem as great. However, a healthy reckoning with a more complete, albeit tarnished, view of history is consistent with CRT and with truth. In order to heal history's wounds, the truth must be told. We can no longer brandish a white supremacist version of history, only telling those parts that make us look good. What we believe about ourselves as a nation matters. This includes church history, the role of professing Christians and slavery, and Christianity's complicity in racism.

MYTH #5: CRT STATES THAT WHITE PEOPLE ARE RACIST

Making anti-racism a synonym for anti-whiteness is another all-too-familiar tactic among CRT's critics, even religious ones.[25] In discussing racism and the Catholic Church, Lawrence Lucas encapsulates CRT's view of white people and racism well: "When I speak of the Catholic Church as a white racist institution, I speak of its group picture, and a group picture does not reflect every individual in the group."[26] Father Lucas was not a CRT theorist, but his explanation of "group picture" parallels CRT's institutional lens. Not all white people are racist; however, most white people benefit from a white-privileged system. Lucas says that "the Catholic Church is a white racist institution: It looks white; it thinks white; it acts white." Even while identifying the Roman Catholic Church in America as a racist institution, Lucas says that to identify all Catholics as racists would not be true. But he requests that white Catholics take a hard, honest look at themselves in hope of realizing positive racial change.

CRT distinguishes between whiteness as a system of power and white people, who may or may not be allies. Ibram X. Kendi, who is not a CRT theorist but an anti-racist scholar and historian, states that there is no neutrality with racism; either you are actively anti-racist or not. If you're not actively opposing racism, you are part of a racist system that contributes to ongoing discrimination, regardless of your personal prejudices or lack thereof. He never states, though, as Ted Cruz has alleged, that "Critical race theory says every white person is a racist." CRT does not state this. This distinction between individual people and institutions is key to grasping CRT, and will be further explored in this book.

MYTH #6: CRT IS INCONSISTENT WITH THE GOSPEL

Among the central themes of the Gospel is liberation from oppression: Liberation of one's heart (salvation), liberation of one's life to be productive and healthy, liberation from death, and liberation of the society in which one lives. The Gospel identifies the oppression (sin) that enmeshes humans and the liberation (salvation) found in the atoning work of Jesus that frees one to love one's neighbor as oneself (equity). The Gospel frees Christians to be used by the Holy Spirit to impact the world and spread that same freedom to others. The Gospel is also about sacrifice and repentance, grace and forgiveness, and being blessed with a spiritually and socially abundant life. The full Gospel usually means salvation, sanctification, divine healing, and Christ's eventual return.

Nothing in CRT contradicts these aspects of the Gospel. It does not even address most of them. But, like the Gospel, CRT envisions the liberation of society from oppression. Jesus was all about liberation. As a Jew, he was oppressed under the domination of the Romans. Defiantly, Jesus spoke out against his oppressors, eventually leading to his state-sponsored execution. His murder demonstrates what Black theologians have understood for centuries: The Bible speaks to both oppressors and the oppressed.

CRT is accused of dividing people into oppressed and oppressors. While this is not the goal of CRT, Christians should be the first to recognize oppression as operative within their societies, for oppressive social structures led to the crucifixion of their Lord. The Old Testament, no less than the New, explores the complexities of oppression. The Book of Exodus focuses on Moses and the liberation of the Hebrew slaves from their Egyptian oppressors.[27] Black slaves in America drew upon these texts to cling to the hope of liberation. Black theologians have used them to denounce white supremacy, white privilege, and Euro-American hegemony. It is not an accident that Martin Luther King Jr. is now called the modern Moses.

Despite how his legacy is portrayed today, King was a CRT theorist before it had that label.[28] King faced massive resistance from both religious and governmental forces, which evinced many of the same tropes as today's anti-CRT propogandists. Those critics often portray CRT as opposed to the teachings of King, but this tactic is yet more evidence of how whitewashed King's legacy has become. White Americans have no problem with the "I Have a Dream" speech, but ignore King's condemnation of militarism, economic injustice, and calls for radical policy reform in housing and wealth distribution. King's Gospel-inspired message of liberation and social equality are congruous with CRT. But after the civil rights era, CRT became another tool for examining how racism operates in society and in our churches. Nothing more, nothing less. There are no inconsistencies here. CRT is not a religion nor a philosophy that undermines Christianity. It is consistent with the Gospel.

ATTACKING CRT BEFORE UNDERSTANDING WHAT IT IS

When this book was being written, Alabama state representative Chris Pringle was trying to pass legislation banning the teaching of CRT. But when asked to define it, he could not provide a definition. When interviewed and asked to name any CRT theorists or to explain the theory, Pringle replied, "Yeah, uh, well—I can assure you—I'll have to read a lot more."[29] Neil Shenvi, a Christian apologist, chemist, and CRT critic, admitted that most Christians are not well-informed about CRT: "Christians, in general, are woefully ill-equipped to accurately represent and critique critical theory because of relying too heavily on secondary sources." Ironically, he goes on to cite *White Fragility* by Robin DiAngelo as necessary first-source reading. DiAngelo is neither a CRT theorist, nor did she write a book based on CRT. It is hardly a primary source. Most CRT critics have not read the seminal works, cannot define CRT to any intelligent degree, and have created their own fabricated definitions.

A critical faith is what is needed. Instead, anti-intellectualism and anti-science biases run deep in many Christian circles. Evangelical historian Mark Noll famously criticized "the evangelical mind" as having become contradictory in terms. "American evangelicals," he wrote, "are not exemplary for their thinking, and they have not been so for several generations."[30] He cites the abandonment of higher education and the life of the mind to the detriment of the church's impact and witness. Catholic priest Lawrence Lucas is more blunt: "The full, horrible truth is that the Church wrecks black minds. This is not unique to the Catholic Church obviously; Christianity in America has hardly been geared to the black man's interests. The most devastating effect of Catholicism on Negroes has been the loss of their minds as black people."[31] Unfortunately, the separation of our minds from our experience of faith can have devastating, long-term consequences. The current battle over race in America is just one of them.

If the attacks on CRT were just a matter of misinformation based on people not doing their intellectual homework, that would be bad enough, but the vitriol around race feels more like anti-Black prejudice and lack of racial empathy. The myths debunked in this chapter are not exhaustive of the attacks rallied against CRT as a theory or the conglomerate of diversity trainings, teachings, and writings that are erroneously labeled as CRT. This theory represents no threat to Western civilization, the church, or children. However, the lack of critical faith and the generational anti-intellectual bent operative in our churches have made members ripe for misinformation and conspiratorial thinking.[32]

It should be no surprise that the current controversy over CRT is yet another result of abandonment of the life of the mind within the American church. Grappling with the complexities of race, racism, ethnicity, and diversity requires deep, nuanced thinking with an understanding of history, psychology, sociology, and theology. Many facets of the American Christian church are ill-prepared for this type of work.

NOTES

1   Stauffer, "When Polarization Hits Pews."
2   Stout, "CRT MAP."
3   Stout.
4   Lesperance, *Critical Race Theory.*
5   Brown, *Critical Race Theory.*
6   Tisby and Moore, *The Color of Compromise.*
7   Brown, *Critical Race Theory.*
8   Avlon, "Martin Luther King, Jr. a Communist?"
9   Quinn, "Are All White People Racist?"
10 Swain, *Pat Robertson and Dr. Swain Discuss Critical Race Theory on the 700 Club.*
11 "DeSantis."
12 Baucham, *Fault Lines.*
13 Barnum, "Busing."
14 Brown, *Critical Race Theory*; Baucham, *Fault Lines*; Strachan and MacArthur, *Christianity and Wokeness.*
15 Baucham.
16 Fischl, "Some Realism."
17 Legg, " Marxist?"

18 Crenshaw, "Essential Reading"; Gordon, "'A Short History."
19 Kristof, "Opinion"
20 Kristof.
21 Bell, *Ethical Ambition*.
22 Griswold, "Tim Wise Defends."
23 Delgado and Stefancic, *Critical Race Theory*; Griswold.
24 Griswold.
25 Crenshaw, "Essential Reading."
26 Lucas, *Black Priest White Church*.
27 Brown, *Critical Race Theory*.
28 Crenshaw, "King Was a Critical Race Theorist."
29 Whitmire, "Lawmaker Wants to Ban."
30 Noll, *The Scandal of the Evangelical Mind*.
31 Noll.
32 Luo, "The Wasting of the Evangelical Mind"; Noll.

CHAPTER THREE

Derrick Bell
The Prophet and Critical Faith

"The dire fate for a prophet is that one preaches, and no one listens;
that one risks all to speak the truth, and nobody cares."

—Derrick Bell

Throughout the CRT controversy, the late Derrick Albert Bell Jr. has been particularly vilified. He's been called radically racist, anti-white, antisemitic, and anti-American. Yet his despisers know little to nothing about him. These attacks on the founder of CRT are egregious because Bell is not alive to defend himself. Nevertheless, his writings and his family, friends, and students continue to speak for him. This chapter will provide a brief account of his life and work, both of which are the target of anti-CRT critiques, but neither of which is commonly understood.

EARLY LIFE

Derrick Albert Bell Jr. was born on November 6, 1930, in Pittsburgh, Pennsylvania, to Derrick Sr. and Ada Bell. His father was a laborer who at one time owned a small rubbish company. Bell Sr. never graduated from high school but would ensure that his children did. According to Bell, his mother was strong in facing injustice and taught her son the dangers of inaction in the face of white dominance and hostility. She once confronted their landlord, who had refused to fix their broken apartment steps. With money in one hand, she went to the rental office to demand management fix the steps so her children would not get hurt. She risked being put out on the street, but instead the landlord fixed the steps and those of their neighbors. Ada Bell was a force to be reckoned with. Bell learned from her example.

By his own admission, the Black church had a strong impact on Bell's life. He attended the African Methodist Episcopal Church as a child. Later he attended an all-Black Presbyterian church led by Rev. Dr. Harold W. Toliver. Bell described him as a Godly man who "convinced him that he was something special."[1] Bell loved singing in the church choir, so much that as an adult and scholar he played gospel music in his home office and titled one of his books *Gospel Choirs: Psalms of Survival in an Alien Land Called Home.*

Bell served in the American military and in the 1950s was a young air force lieutenant stationed in Louisiana. One Sunday he wished to attend church, but the local Presbyterian churches were for white people only. Bell dressed in his military uniform, went to the white church, and asked to attend worship. The surprised and outraged ushers gave him a pew by himself in the balcony. But he did not stop there. He later asked the minister if he could sing in the choir. He could not accept that the church would segregate him to the balcony and bar him from singing for the Lord because of the color of his skin. This incident was one of many where he confronted discrimination in bigoted institutions.[2]

The eldest of four siblings, Bell was the first in his family to go to college. He attended Duquesne University in Pittsburgh and was a member of the US Army Reserve Officer Training Corps, graduating in 1952 with a bachelor's degree. He then received a Bachelor of Law from the University of Pittsburgh Law School in 1957, where he was the only Black student and was elected an associate editor-in-chief of the school *Law Review.*[3]

His law career included time in the US Justice Department as one of the few Black attorneys in the civil rights division, but he was forced to resign for refusing to relinquish his NAACP membership. Later he was recruited and hired by Thurgood Marshall to head the Pittsburgh NAACP Legal Defense and Educational Fund, working on projects that included the integration of recreational parks, swimming pools, and skating facilities. He labored under dangerous conditions in Mississippi as a civil rights lawyer, overseeing more than 300 school desegregation cases during the 1960s. The early lessons from his mother and the Louisiana church propelled him to push the status quo and use ethical confrontation against discrimination; they would drive his writing, thinking, and actions in challenging racist institutions.

After his death in 2011, he was attacked by Hannity on the Fox News Channel, Breitbart News Network, and former Alaska governor Sarah Palin for his association with his former Harvard law student, Barack Obama. He was lambasted for supporting Obama's intellectual development and derided as a racial radical, an antisemite, and an anti-American communist.[4] His widow responded to these accusations:

My husband was a war veteran. And he was a patriot. And what he tried to do is make this country stand up to the ideals that he believed in. He believed it with his whole heart. Derrick thought that the ideals of fair play, social justice, equality, opportunity—those are things that should be shared. Everybody should get a shot at the American dream. That is what Derrick Bell was about.[5]

SPEAKING TRUTH TO POWER

Despite his vast on-the-ground civil rights work, Bell is best known for his university scholarship, beginning in 1966 at the University of Southern California, then at Harvard Law School, where he served as the first tenured African American professor of law in 1971. From 1980 to 1985, he was dean of the University of Oregon School of Law, and then from 1991 until his death in 2011, he was a visiting professor at New York University School of Law.[6]

His ethics and commitment to addressing injustice followed him his entire academic career. The University of Oregon School of Law was a bastion of white male dominance, not unlike other universities, and Bell worked tirelessly to hire women and people of color to address this imbalance. He quit when the school's faculty refused to honor his recommendation to hire Pat K. Chew, a Chinese American woman, who was at the time a corporate associate at a major San Francisco law firm. Oregon's law school had a large Asian and women student enrollment, but no faculty representation. Chew, a highly qualified candidate, was rejected. Bell resigned in protest.

After quitting Oregon, Bell returned to Harvard. He said Harvard "was the best job in the world," and that he had colleagues and friends of all races on the faculty, even though they came from diverse life experiences and held disparate opinions on many issues.[7] But in 1987, similar discriminatory hiring practices emerged at Harvard. In response, Bell organized a protest on campus to bring attention to the university's failure to grant tenure to two white professors, Claire Dalton and David Trubek, whose scholarship engaged the critical legal studies movement.[8] Barack Obama, while studying at Harvard, joined Bell in protesting the lack of minority hiring, particularly the failure to grant tenure to African American professor Regina Austin. Critics of the former president and CRT drew attention to a 1990 demonstration where Obama and Bell protested together.

On April 24, 1990, Bell announced that he would take an unpaid leave of absence from Harvard until at least one woman of color was appointed to the law school on a full-time basis. He had often been the lone faculty protester with his students, exercising his constitutional right of protest at the cost of extreme personal and professional sacrifice. His protest cost him a tenured position at one of the most prestigious universities in the world.[9]

WRITING AS ACTIVISM

Bell was a prolific writer, and his writing was itself an act of protest. He wrote twelve books, including his now classic casebook *Race, Racism, and American Law,* now in its sixth edition and used in law schools across the country. In addition, he wrote countless ground-breaking articles cited by tens of thousands of scholars.

Beyond traditional academic writing, Bell wrote science fiction short stories, allegories, and parables in the style of C. S. Lewis to illustrate his legal positions on race. His academic writing is peppered with fiction, the scriptures, and African American spirituals. His critics claimed that his storytelling was inappropriate for academia, and yet his writings on race in American law have made him one of the most influential legal scholars of his generation.[10] Bell disturbed both conservative and liberal segments of academia through his protests and writing, challenging the idea that significant progress on race in America had occurred. He claimed that the civil rights movement had not met its goals; in fact, the country was losing ground on race relations. He had been in the struggle during the movement, so he saw hard-won gains being eroded. CRT was in part a response to this erosion.

TEACHING

Derrick Bell is rightfully remembered for his university protests and scholarship on CRT, but it was his teaching that he most valued and that his students most applauded. In preparation for this chapter, I talked to former students and read reports from multiple others. Bell taught with his whole being: investing time, opening his home, listening, advising, and following students in their careers. He was original and creative in his approach to teaching, diverging from the classic law school Socratic method that interrogates students. His community-based classroom used a participatory pedagogical approach to teach constitutional law; it engaged students deeply and placed them at the center of the learning process. This method, rooted in John Dewey and Paulo Freire, was no less rigorous than the more traditional methods.[11]

Bell taught until the week before he died of carcinoid cancer at the age of eighty. He inspired students to work for social change and to reach their full potential in all aspects of their lives. He once said, "My relationships with students have been the most satisfying part of my teaching career," and that love translated to the students at Harvard giving him glowing evaluations.[12] He was a teacher and mentor for hundreds. He was beloved by students of all races and backgrounds.[13]

In the words of Patricia J. Williams, Bell's former student and now the University Distinguished Professor of Law and Humanities at Northeastern University:

> I met Professor Derrick Albert Bell when I was nineteen years old. . . . At that point in my life, I was thinking of going on for a PhD in . . . linguistics? Urban studies? Sociology? Maybe art history. I was lost in the something-or-other stage of my life and couldn't for the life of me make up my squishy, floaty mind.
>
> Professor Bell's lecture fixed all that. He had that class divided into interest and advocacy groups, taking various sides in the Supreme Court cases they were studying. The teams were arguing with each other like mad, and the passion and purpose flying around that room were like tangible objects. You had to duck to avoid getting laser-beamed by the sharp, whizzing commotion of high-octane ideas. . . . He made ideas come alive. He made the dry pages of treatises vivid; he never let us forget the human stories behind every tract, every suit, every appeal. He imbued legal education with a sense of purpose and responsibility: we weren't there for ourselves alone, but to live up to a calling and to become of service. He helped me reframe the sense of isolation and intimidation I felt.[14]

Elliott Dawes, a former student who later became the original director of the NYC Black Male Initiative Program, noted:

> I was in Professor Bell's Basic Constitutional Law course and . . . learned more in one course with Bell than an entire year of constitutional law courses. . . . [I]n some classes you would be afraid to speak—it was the exact opposite in Bell's course; there was so much dialogue. He was patient, a real teacher, fantastic teacher. [He] facilitated discussion even with students who opposed him; he did not shut down discussions. [He was] welcoming, [and had] humor [and] respect for everyone. Once there were conservative students and [he] treated them with complete respect. [There were] lots of civil rights cases he talked about; [he] told stories from his own experience. One time I walked with him to his office and we walked down a stairwell and stood there talking for an hour or two. It was a teaching moment. He was spontaneous; he liked people and wanted to see people succeed professionally and personally. He was prepared to teach his classes while writing prolifically.[15]

Bell's students described him as a gentle, kind, funny, and caring man who courageously acted on his convictions. Three hundred signed an open letter in support of Bell's legacy following the recent onslaught to disparage CRT and Bell:

> This Open Letter is in support of Professor Bell's legacy as a highly respected colleague, advocate and mentor. We disavow any efforts to discredit Professor Bell, to malign his character, or to mischaracterize his contributions. We recognize Derrick Bell as a great champion of equality for all Americans. We honor his legacy and the example he provided of a life fully and courageously lived.

> First, he taught us that the legal academy is inert when people of color, women of color, and critical voices are excluded. Second,

he taught us that each of us can choose to confront authority, or we can acquiesce. Sometimes, it will not be enough to notice, complain about, or even write about an injustice. Sometimes, life requires that we take a stand. But finally, and best of all, Professor Bell reminded us that one person's actions can make a difference.[16]

HIS FAITH

After a valiant battle with cancer, Derrick Bell died on October 5, 2011. He died a man of incredibly deep faith. His now-retired pastor and fellow civil rights activist, Dr. Paul Smith of the First Presbyterian Church of Brooklyn, stated that the Bible verse best suited to sum up Bell's extraordinary life is "Well done, good and faithful servant."[17] Reverend Smith described an experience that happened several weeks before Bell died:

A couple of weeks before Derrick died, I went to his home as I have done on several occasions, but this particular day Derrick was a bit agitated because of his bouts with pain. He spoke softly that evening and when I asked him a question, he instead asked me "to offer prayer." I took his hand in mine and after a long silence, I began our prayer. As I prayed with Derrick he closed his eyes and soon fell asleep. . . . It was a sacramental moment for me, and I will remember our experience for many years to come.[18]

Bell's faith not only was an anchor for him in death, but provided support and hope amid the ongoing frustrations of working for racial justice. Bell wrote:

I have relied on my faith. Particularly in hard times, my Christian faith provides reassurance that is unseen but no less real. It never fails to give me the fortitude I need when opposing injustice despite the almost certain failure of my action to persuade those in authority to alter their plans or policies. For me it is my most powerful resource.[19]

Bell's faith guided his beliefs and actions, even outside the strictures of church structure and official doctrine. Priest Richard Rohr calls this an experience of the true self and of the mystery of Christ, which is not the same as institutionalized Christianity.[20] Simultaneously, Bell appears to have been a regular church member committed to the institution of church. Bell's approach to Christianity rejected fundamentalism but kept its spirit. In his books, he referred often to doing God's work. In addition, Bell drew deeply upon music and the message of spirituals and gospel hymns. He called this "theology in song."[21] He established an annual gospel choir concert at NYU. In 2009, the event was titled "Evolving Faith in an Uncertain World." Designed to provide inspirational strength to students and faculty to overcome challenges of all kinds, this concert quickly became a tradition at NYU School of Law. His aim was to provide spiritual support and reassurance to the law school community.

CRT is criticized for being pessimistic, as it states that racism is endemic and permanent in America. Yet Bell's faith contradicts this assertion. To explain this seeming contradiction, you can look at racism just as you look at sin. Sin is an ever-present phenomenon in humans, yet we strive to repent and transform. Much like sin, racism is permanent, yet does not preclude actions to alter these conditions. Bell's spirituality is vital to understanding how we work for change despite racism's permeation through society. Faith requires work in the world. One of the most frequently cited Bible verses in Bell's writing is "So faith by itself, if it has no works, is dead."[22] Bell knew that faith was essential in the Black community's struggle for racial justice.[23]

His faith was evident to some of his students. He professed it subtly, tactfully, and with wisdom that was neither divisive nor inappropriate. His student, Keith Boykin, a writer and broadcaster, described Bell's faith:

Professor Bell was fond of quoting biblical scriptures [African-American] spirituals and gospel hymns in his books and in his classroom lectures. When I took his not-for-credit class during his leave of absence protest at Harvard Law School in the 1990–91 school year, it felt as though I was being taught by a preacher as much as an ivy league professor. Indeed, Derrick Bell was both. Although he was a man of strong conviction, he was also a gentle soul who spoke softly and kindly and smiled broadly. What drew him to the teachings of Christ, he once wrote, was Jesus's "courage and vision of radical inclusiveness."[24]

Bell was a devoted husband, a proud father of three sons, and a mentor to many "adopted" sons and daughters from all walks of life. He was an advocate for women's rights, LGBTQ rights, and disability rights long before these became popular causes. Bell did all this with great love. He showed us that we retain our humanity through our relationships with each other, even those with whom we disagree.[25] He lived a full life, exuding joy amid the struggles. His wife states, "We lived such a full and joyous life in the midst—in the midst of the struggle. He made struggle very attractive."[26] The fruits of the Spirit were evident in his life.

BELL THE PROPHET

In the Bible there are priests and there are prophets. Prophets are less popular because they critique society and institutions, calling for change. The most credible prophets are those who work and speak from within those institutions. The prophetic path challenges us not to avoid evil, pain, and fear in the world, but rather to turn to the world with compassion. Usually, prophets are laypeople like Jesus or Moses, who dared by their own inner authority from God to critique the institutions within which they lived.[27] Through their experience, prophets speak truth to power. Within the church, there is very little reason to oppose priests because they maintain the status quo, whereas prophets challenge it, often at great cost to their lives. This is the process of systems refining themselves from within. We need both priests and prophets.[28]

Derrick Bell is a prophet by this measure, although he never called himself one. Bell never spoke directly to the institution of the church, but he spoke to the legal, economic, and social systems of America. Derrick Bell, from within the legal system and the academy, critiqued both conservatives and liberals when it came to legal policies centered around race. He critiqued from within systems that he loved and participated in—academia, the military, and the church. Reflecting on this process, he wrote, "There is something of the Moses within each of us that we must offer as a service, as a living sacrifice to those like ourselves."[29] As Rohr argues, "Prophets ... put together the best of the conservative with the best of the liberal, to use contemporary language. They honor the tradition, and they also say what's phony about the tradition. That is what fully spiritually mature people can do."[30]

Bell was grounded in Christianity, yet provocative and unsettling in his writing, his views, and his actions. Bell at one point challenged the institution of the church with the accusations that most racists are also Christians.[31] He was performing the role of a prophet. Bell was an insider, a Christian, and a church member speaking with authority as a layman and as a scholar. "While striving to do the Lord's work," Bell wrote, "we will look to many of our adversaries and some of our friends like the devil incarnate."[32] He referred to racial struggle as the work of Moses and to Black people and anti-racists as a race of Jeremiahs, prophets calling for the nation to repent. Prophets in the Bible were Israel's conscience. Bell believed that Black people and anti-racists in America are the nation's conscience:

Listen: it is the black American who puts pressure upon the nation to live up to its ideals. It is he who gives creative tension to our struggle for justice and for the elimination of those factors, social and psychological, which make for slums and shaky suburban communities.... Without the black American, something irrepressibly hopeful and creative would go out of the American spirit, and the nation might well succumb to the moral snobbism that has ever threatened its existence from within.[33]

Despite his strong critiques, Bell had no illusions of infallibility. He was quick to say that he or anyone can be wrong even when thinking they are right. He learned this lesson the hard way during his civil rights work in Harmony, Mississippi, with Winson and Dovie Hudson, two determined sisters and local civil rights workers who risked their lives, jobs, and friends to bring equity to their community. Bell won a case for the desegregation of Harmony, Mississippi, schools in 1964, which resulted in the closing of a historic and excellent Black school. Bell and the Hudsons had reason to regret some of these legal actions, which, in retrospect, did more harm than good to the Black community.[34] In Bell's words:

> The protester, while seeking always to carry the banner of truth and justice, must remember that the fires of commitment do not bestow the gift of infallibility. Even the most well-meaning can err in the mission of good, can worsen conditions they seek to reform.[35]

Bell was a man of faith, a loving husband and father, a committed teacher to all his students, a prolific writer, a courageous civil rights lawyer, a humble prophet, and an originator of CRT. He displayed an aspect of critical faith that identifies evil and speaks to institutions with the goal of rooting out that evil. As James said, "Faith without works is dead." Bell's faith was alive and well.

NOTES

1 Bell, *Confronting Authority.*
2 Butterfield, "Old Rights Campaigner."
3 Bernstein, "Derrick Bell, Law Professor."
4 Hannity, "Obama Can Sleep"; Adams, "Obama's Beloved Law Professor."

5 "The Ed Show."
6 MasterClass, "Derrick Bell."
7 Bell, *Confronting Authority.*
8 Butler et al., "The Story. "
9 Bell, *Confronting Authority.*
10 Butler et al., "The Story."
11 Radice, "Community-Based Classroom."
12 Bell, *Confronting Authority.*
13 "The Ed Show."
14 "Rev. Dr. Paul Smith."
15 Dawes, Elliott. Interview by Joni Schwartz-Chaney. November 21, 2022.
16 Butler et al., "The Story. "
17 Mt 25:23.
18 "Rev. Dr. Paul Smith."
19 Bell, *Ethical Ambition.*
20 Rohr, *Immortal Diamond.*
21 Taylor, "Racism as 'The Nation's Crucial Sin.'"
22 James 2:14–26 (New International Version).
23 Taylor, "Race, Religion, and Law."
24 Boykin, "Derrick Bell Official Site."
25 Butler et al., "The Story. "
26 "The Ed Show for Monday, March 12, 2012."
27 Rohr, *Immortal Diamond.*
28 Rohr.
29 Bell, *Faces at the Bottom.*
30 Rohr, *Immortal Diamond.*
31 Taylor, "Racism as 'The Nation's Crucial Sin'"; Taylor, "Race, Religion, and Law."
32 Bell, *Faces at the Bottom.*
33 Bell.
34 Winson Hudson and Constance Curry, *Mississippi Harmony.*
35 Bell, *Faces at the Bottom.*

CHAPTER FOUR

Defining Race and Racism

"We are all related, more than seven billion of us, distant cousins to one another, and, ultimately, everyone is African."

—Daniel J. Fairbanks

Thinking about race, talking about race, and ultimately tackling racism all require deep thinking. American Christians too often avoid the intellectual labor necessary for grappling with this deep-seated issue. White Christians use ignorance to disengage. During the civil rights movement, a majority of white evangelicals, Catholics, and mainline Protestants were either silent or responded with disdain when called upon by Martin Luther King Jr. and other Black clergy to support the movement.[1] The Black church did the heavy lifting, sacrifice, and intellectual work.[2]

Admitting this failure to show up is a good place to begin the deep work that the study of race in America requires. Defining what race is and what it isn't is crucial. Varying perceptions of race abound, and the confusion about CRT is yet another example. These differing definitions are loaded with emotion. *Race* is a word we were taught not to bring up in polite company, unless we wanted to make people uncomfortable; I have found this particularly true in the company of white people. At social gatherings, if someone asks me what I write about and I say, "Race," there is frequently an uncomfortable silence and the conversation shuts down. But the conversation is too important to abandon. This chapter will attempt to provide working definitions of race and racism so that the conversation can finally begin.

DEFINING RACE AND ETHNICITY

Race is a social construct. This phrase is used inside and outside the church. But what does it mean, and what is the evidence that it is true? *A social construct* is an idea created by people in a society. Once a concept is embraced by members of a group, it becomes part of the cultural thinking and perception. It is modeled, taught, and unconsciously ingrained from birth through old age, becoming a normal part of society's way of seeing itself.

One example of a social construct is the way a society sees animals as either pets or food. Guinea pigs are pets in America, but in other countries are served along with fruits and vegetables at dinnertime. Biologically, the animals are identical. But what that biology *means* varies across cultures, each creating and applying distinct meanings to these animals. Beauty is another social construct. Societies collectively decide what is attractive, and these conventions change over time. Social constructs evolve with changing norms.

Race is a powerful and long-lasting social construct. Despite overwhelming scientific proof to the contrary, many individuals still believe that race is biological and that human beings can be divided into racial categories—despite the fact that none of these categories exist in biological reality. They are social constructs. We use these cultural lenses to see Asian, brown, Black, and white races when they are not real.

Race is not the same as ethnicity or ancestry. Race is the dividing and social ascribing of people into groups based on physical characteristics (skin color, facial features, hair texture, etc.), but ethnicity refers to peoples in geographic regions. It includes shared language, heritage, religions, and social customs. Ancestry is one's family origin or ethnic descent. Ancestry is arguably the most accurate way of classifying groups of people from within the methods and parameters of biology and population dynamics.

People of the same ethnicity can be of different races—as seen, for example, among Latino people. But once those differences in skin tone take on cultural or societal meaning and become attached to hierarchies, we've gone beyond biology and into the social construct called *colorism*. Although even the US Census Bureau uses racial markers in its surveys (white, Black or African American, Asian, American Indian and Alaska Native, Native Hawaiian and Pacific Islander, and other), it is not measuring what many people think it is. The result is a woefully inaccurate mixture of ancestral, ethnic, and racial categories, and not a reality that exists in nature.[3]

RACE IS NOT REAL

What does it mean to say that these categories are not real? No racial classifications exist in science. Races are not biological. And science cannot verify race because there is no racial root in our biological DNA, biological anthropology, or archaeological science. Science proves repeatedly and rigorously that race does not exist. We now understand that humans are 99.9 percent genetically identical, so genetic science cannot divide us into races. Human geneticists and scientists from across disciplines are now curbing their use of the word *race* in their writing and scholarly work because it scientifically does not exist. We have constructed the concept of race based on a combination of ideology, imagination, and mythical thinking.

There is a problem, however. In our everyday lived experience, we know that race exists. It exists in how we see the world. It exists because we see it, refer to it, use it to classify people, write books about it, pass legislation having to do with it, and become emotional about it. We distinguish between Black churches and white churches, and Black history and American history. We identify ourselves and others by race. For something that is not real, it seems to really matter. From the insistence that race is not biologically real must follow the recognition that race is all too real in its impact on the world. Race is real in that societies use it to build and distribute resources, privileges, and rights.[4] Race works as a powerful lie with powerful effects in economics, education, health decisions, employment, criminal justice, housing determinations, and countless other spheres of social life.

Race and racism are not interchangeable. Race as a social creation sets up structures of domination and power based on essentialist categories.[5] Racism occurs either on a personal level or institutional level, wherein one ascribed group assumes superiority over another to the detriment of all. Prejudice and discrimination occur through the unjust power of one race over another. CRT is particularly useful in elaborating how this happens in a society and through its institutions (more on institutional racism in Chapter 7). CRT helps us understand how racism permeates society in seemingly invisible ways.

HUMAN GENOME PROJECT

Francis Collins, an evangelical Christian, was a lead scientist for the National Human Genome Project, a groundbreaking international and collaborative genetics project that established that race has no biological basis.[6] A renowned American physician-geneticist, Collins launched the American portion of the project in 1990 and completed it in 2003, working alongside some of the most brilliant scientists in the world. The Human Genome Institute continues building on the discoveries of its original project. The results of this collaborative research made a wealth of knowledge available to clinicians, epidemiologists, and public health responders during the Ebola and Covid-19 pandemics and provided the science to manufacture the pandemic vaccines. (Collins was also the NIH director during the Ebola pandemic and early days of the Covid pandemic.)

This project employed the world's best scientists to sequence the DNA in human cells. Its consequent medical and biotechnical advances have been extraordinary, including the discovery of genetic testing for predisposition to cancer, Alzheimer's, sickle cell anemia, Down syndrome, and liver diseases. Its results have also led to advances in the fields of criminal justice, adoption, and paternity queries. Prisoners wrongly convicted can be proven innocent using DNA, while those same technologies can be used to identify the actual culprits. Ancestory.com and other ancestry investigations have reunited families and settled paternity suits. Controversially, genetic testing for ancestry services were used to identify Joseph James DeAngelo as the Golden State Killer, a serial murderer who avoided capture for decades.

Through the Human Genome Project, scientists achieved a high-quality sequencing of the entire human genome, 2.85 billion nucleotides, with a predicted error rate of just one event in every 100,000 bases sequenced.[7] Its findings continue to have important implications for biomedical research and cures for inherited diseases to this day. We now know that racial diseases do not exist and that racial differences in IQ are the result of socioeconomic conditions and education quality rather than genetic differences.[8] The Human Genome Project corroborated what archaeological and biological research had previously indicated—race does not exist biologically, and there is no scientific basis for current racial categories.[9] Interestingly, the project also confirmed that we are all African by origin.

WE ARE ALL AFRICAN

The Human Genome Project ascertained that humans originated in Africa roughly 250,000 years ago.[10] Every person alive today could, in principle, trace their genetic ancestry to Africa. Independently of genomic researchers, archaeologists came to the same conclusion. No longer do the world's scientists question the findings.[11] A consensus has been reached, although ongoing research suggests that modern humans evolved from various locations in Africa, not just one as originally thought.[12]

Our early ancestors left Africa between 60,000 and 70,000 years ago, migrating to Europe, Asia, and beyond. Since "there are no discrete genetic boundaries separating so-called races" and the over-whelming scientific evidence traces the human origins to Africa, identifying one's ancestry is more scientifically accurate than identifying race.[13] If our social problems with race were a function of biology, this scientific evidence should settle the race question and eliminate racism once and for all. With science unifying us as one "race" with differing ancestral stories, racism should no longer exist. Yet, despite these scientific discoveries, race and racism endure. The history of racism is long and has left its impact.[14]

Fundamentalist and literalist Christianity attribute the origin of the human species to Adam and Eve, our first parents, who lived in a garden in what is now Iraq. Particularly in America, decades of fundamentalist rejection of science has resulted in the maintaining of a literal reading of the creation story and a rejection of evolution. A resurgence in the 1960s of a creation science movement in some parts of the church is still active. According to historian and writer Mark Noll, the great tragedy of modern creationism is that it drowns out the intelligent and careful Christian thinkers and scientists, who balance a faith in God with science to forge a critical faith. These are Christians who understand that God reveals Himself or Herself through nature, the human body, and the Bible.[15]

Some Christians mixed fundamentalist theology with claims that Adam and Eve were the original parents of the white race, while other races evolved from animals. The long-term result of this theology and the invention of race was religious justification for colonialism and for treating certain groups as chattel. Even today, extreme right-wing groups affiliated with portions of the church talk about racial purity. There are some who still embrace notions of separatism. White nationalist groups such as the KKK, neo-confederates, neo-Nazis, and racist skinheads claim Christian identity. Antisemitic, racist theology provides religious cover for violence and domestic terrorism. American far-right extremism holds onto dangerous and erroneous social constructions. Despite scientific evidence that refutes the existence of racial categories, the classification of people is burdened with a long, horrific history centering white supremacy and the exercise of control for economic gain.[16]

THE CURSE OF HAM

Genesis 9:18–19 tells the story of Noah getting drunk and falling asleep naked. Noah's son Ham discovers his father's state and tells his two brothers, Shem and Japheth, who then cover their father with a blanket. For reasons unexplained, Ham's son Canaan is cursed, and Noah prophecies that Ham's family will be the lowest of servants and slaves to the descendants of Shem and Japheth. During medieval times, there emerged the belief that dark-skinned people were the descendants of Ham, because he had dark skin according to some translations. To justify slavery in America, these passages were offered as proof that slavery was the fulfillment of prophecy. The Black race was deemed morally and intellectually inferior because of the curse of Ham, only to be redeemed within the master–slave relationship. According to this interpretation, God sanctioned and ordained slavery because Africans were slated by God to live under its bondage. This tradition, unfortunately, outlived slavery itself.

Louis T. Talbot, an evangelical minister, author, and president and founder of Biola University and Talbot School of Theology in Los Angeles, wrote a fair amount about race, interracial marriage, and the Curse of Ham. He wrote that "God has stamped [Black people] with characteristics which forever distinguish them from other races—characteristics of which color is only one. And it is not by chance that the [Black people] have been 'a servant of servants.' This fact is but prophecy fulfilled."[17]

Talbot believed the Hamitic Curse that Black people were ordained by God to be slaves and their oppression was prophesied in the Bible.

When responding to the question of integration, separation of races, and interracial marriage, Talbot stated:

> Personally, I think [Black people] are far happier with their own race. Furthermore, I am convinced that God intended that it should be so, and that the two races should not intermarry.[18]

Talbot opposed interracial marriage on the basis of his interpretation of Genesis 9:25 and preached this racist view. A well-respected evangelist and Bible college president, Talbot died in 1976. Unfortunately, as recent as 2014, the reprint of his book, *Bible Questions Explained,* contains these same racist interpretations. There are no redactions or editorial commentary explaining why these racist statements are retained in the 2014 edition. To be fair, many modern Christian conservative theologians and writers have backed away from this understanding of race and racism. Still, its influence runs deep within today's churches.

DEFINING RACISM AS SIN

Racism has been called America's *original sin,* and white racism is its legacy. "The United States of America," writes Jim Wallis, "was established as a white society, founded upon the near genocide of another race and then the enslavement of yet another."[19] It can manifest individually (personal acts of microaggressions) or collectively (systemic sin enmeshed within our institutions). Both manifestations are often hidden, tolerated, or denied. Like all types of sin, the remedy is exposure and confession, which make room for transformation.

The Bible addresses sin with the truth: "And the truth shall set you free." This is the effectiveness of CRT as a theory; it aids us in getting at the truth—through the lived experiences of people of color. It also uncovers the racism we tolerate within our policies and institutions. The SBC's Resolution on Critical Race Theory and Intersectionality identifies the role of CRT: "Critical race theory and intersectionality alone are insufficient to diagnose and redress the root causes of the social ills that they identify, which result from sin, yet these analytical tools can aid in evaluating a variety of human experiences."[20]

To their credit, the Southern Baptists acknowledged the usefulness of CRT while stating that CRT is not intended to replace, diagnose, or be a substitute for the Gospel and the Bible's perspective on sin. CRT is a theory that can assist in uncovering truth about American history. A hard truth is that most of our founding fathers were slaveholders, and most "white people, white Christians, and white churches tolerated slavery in North America for 246 years, from 1619 to 1865." In the Reconstruction and post-Reconstruction eras, most white churches and white Christians either supported or tolerated Jim Crow laws and were passive in the civil rights movement. These sins are of a collective and societal nature. So as individual sin finds us out, harms our entire being, and eventually corrupts the whole body, so collective sin corrupts a nation.

Confession is the spiritual anecdote for individual sin. As a child, I knelt in a confessional box and closed a curtain before a barred window. The priest was seen as a shadow through the bars. I confessed my childhood sins, and he absolved me. He then instructed me to pray and lament my sins. I was to go to the offended person, apologize, and make things right. Not bad advice.

The scriptures call us to this kind of confession—an admittance that our national past, spattered with the blood of two genocides, still reverberates in modern institutionalized racism. We as a nation cannot run from this admission or whitewash history. And once it's acknowledged, we must lament.[21] Our churches are places where both confession and lamentation should occur. Confession and lamentation can be freeing—because the truth will set us free. That freedom then moves us to repentance and reparation. *Repentance* means a turning away from the sin, and *reparations* is repairing the wrong such sins cause.

In 1995, the Southern Baptists began the process of confession and apology with the following statement: "We apologize to all

African Americans for condoning and/or perpetuating individual and systemic racism in our lifetime, and we genuinely repent of racism of which we have been guilty, whether consciously or unconsciously."[22] The SBC came to this determination from the scriptures and responded with a confession of sin. It bears repeating, especially in the context of theological statements about corporate sin, that CRT does not itself identify sin or label actions as sinful. Instead, "evangelical scholars who affirm the authority and sufficiency of scripture have employed selective insights from critical race theory . . . to understand [the] multifaceted social dynamics [of racism]."[23] This nontheological tool is helpful to the church as it seeks to identify its sins in theological terms.

The Southern Baptists are not alone in defining racism as sin and moving to confession and repentance. Here is a portion of the Evangelical Lutheran Church in America's (ELCA) Anti-Racism Pledge: "As church we are called to confess the sin of racism, condemn the ideology of white supremacy, and strive for racial justice and peace. Beyond statements and prayers, we are called to also act and respond to injustices." Both the SBC and ECLA have defined racism in *collective* terms as sin, and thus as requiring confession and action according not to a secular theory of justice, but to the spiritual and moral demands of their biblical traditions. This is refreshing because, generally, Christians restrict moral vision around racism to the personal and interpersonal arenas, identifying the root evil in poor relationships between individuals rather than in unfair laws or institutional behavior. According to a well-known Emerson and Smith study about church and race, white evangelicals hold a deep suspicion of systemic solutions and explanations for social problems. They believe that the blame lies with sinful individuals and are reluctant to admit collective guilt.[24] In this regard, the SBC and ECLA break the mold and employ a CRT analysis to identify and understand the churches' racism as collective sin.

Beyond confession, repentance, and contrition is reparation. Collective sin, after all, requires a collective response. Reparations are the restitution for the wrongs committed. Lenny Duncan, in his honest letter to his ECLA community, says he believes reparations come first: "Before reconciliation, before forgiveness, after the acknowledgment of sin, there is something that is groaning to be born in the womb that is the church: reparations."[25] According to Duncan, the church's twenty-first-century calling must be to dismantle white supremacy. It should take inspiration from South Africa's Truth and Reconciliation Commission, where "sinners could face their accusers" and reparations could be requested. Reparations is a theological concept drawn from the biblical principle of atonement for sin, a principle described in Leviticus 5:45–46. Mari Matsuda, a founding practitioner of CRT, has written about legal reparations that the church can learn from: "The reparations concept serves the goal of retribution. The decision to award reparations is an act of contrition and humility that can ease victims' bitterness and alienation . . . and strengthen the social order."[26] Precedent exists for legal reparations. There have been reparations to Native Americans for the loss of territory and genocide; German relocation reparations to Jews so they could migrate to Israel after World War II; the Japanese American Evacuation Claims Act of 1948, which provided some reparations, however inadequate.[27] What would reparations look like in church?

On Sunday morning May 4, 1969, James Forman, then president of the Student Nonviolent Coordinating Committee, hijacked the pulpit of Riverside Church in New York City and read a Black manifesto demanding five hundred million dollars from white churches and synagogues; the act catapulted reparations to media attention. In the years that followed, some churches and denominations gave several million dollars to social programs in Black churches.[28] It is encouraging that more churches, including but not limited to Episcopal, Methodist, and Lutheran congregations, are committing themselves to programs of reparations. The National Council of Churches created a "Faith and Facts" sheet for the Commission to Study and Develop Reparations Proposal for African Americans Act, H.R. 40 designed to end racism.[29] The Jesuits who founded Georgetown University have also pledged $27 million in money and land donations in reparations to each descendant of Black people that the university enslaved and sold, and although the reparations plan has come under some criticism in its execution and fundraising, it is still a template for other religious institutions.[30]

CRT does not specifically demand reparations, although Derrick Bell has a chapter on "The Racial Barriers to Reparations" in *And We Are Not Saved: The Elusive Quest for Racial Justice* and discusses the obstacles today to a "forty acres and a mule" plan of the 1860s,[31] which was designed to provide compensation for slave labor to freed families after the Civil War but never materialized to any major extent. However, CRT is an activist theory working across disciplines with civil rights and social activist scholars to bring about racial justice. Both CRT and reparations are consistent with biblical principles, the culmination of repentance, and justice for the oppressed.

CRITICAL THINKING ABOUT SCIENCE AND RACE

The science that defines race as a social construct is irrefutable. Today scientists from all disciplines agree race has no biological meaning. W. E. B. Du Bois was right in arguing for a sociohistorical definition of race and articulating the lived experience of Blackness in a time when race was defined biologically. Du Bois was a scientific forerunner of the current social construction definition of race and inspired the thinking of CRT theorists.[32] Scientists are phasing out categories of Black and white as biological descriptors. We know, though, that racial categories are necessary in the social and political sciences to understand structural inequalities and discrimination in healthcare, housing, criminal justice, and education, as well as the economic inequalities inherent in racism. Distinguishing one realm of meaning from the other is hard but necessary work.

The church needs to do this hard work as well, and doing so will require critical thinking about the science of race. Herein lie potential obstacles. As previously noted, the American church has an uneasy relationship with science. Rather than seeing science as another window from which to understand the wonders of God and God's work in the world, science is perceived as an adversary—climate change, evolution, and vaccines are examples. Especially in fundamentalist factions of the church, suspicion pervades to this day. If some of the church's kneejerk reactions to CRT are any indication, science may again be seen as foe rather than friend. Critical faith is needed to understand the complexities of race and racism as we use the mind for Christ. President Biden said, "the soul of the Nation is at stake" today in our current racial climate. If that is true—and I have every reason to believe it is—then the remedy for healing the soul is not politics, economics, or even education, but a church possessed of a critical faith.

NOTES

1 Luther King, *Letter from a Birmingham Jail.*
2 Noll, *The Scandal of the Evangelical Mind.*
3 Omi and Winant, *Racial Formation in the United States.*
4 Dyson, *Tears We Cannot Stop.*
5 Omi and Winant, *Racial Formation in the United States.*
6 Collins, *The Language of God.*
7 National Institutes of Health, "15 Ways."
8 Fairbanks, *Everyone Is African.*
9 Collins, *The Language of God*; Mccann-Mortimer, Augoustinos, and Lecouteur, "'Race' and the Human Genome Project."
10 National Institutes of Health, "15 Ways."
11 Fairbanks, *Everyone Is African.*
12 Collins, *The Language of God*; Pérez Ortega, "Human Geneticists."
13 Fairbanks, *Everyone Is African.*
14 Mccann-Mortimer, Augoustinos, and Lecouteur, "'Race' and the Human Genome Project."
15 Noll, *The Scandal of the Evangelical Mind.*
16 Fairbanks, *Everyone Is African.*
17 Talbot, *Bible Questions Explained.*
18 Talbot.
19 Wallis and Stevenson, *America's Original Sin.*
20 Wallis and Stevenson.
21 Rah and McNeil, *Prophetic Lament.*
22 SBC, "Resolution on Racial Reconciliation."
23 SBC, "On Critical Race Theory."
24 Emerson and Smith, *Divided by Faith.*

25 Duncan, *Dear Church.*
26 Matsuda, "Looking to the Bottom."
27 Bell, *And We Are Not Saved.*
28 Bell.
29 National Council of Churches, "Faith and Facts."
30 Swarns, "Catholic Order Pledges."
31 Bell, *And We Are Not Saved.*
32 Avshalom-Smith, "Du Bois and Critical Race."

CHAPTER FIVE

The Past Lives in the Present

"Remembering is our greatest power."

—Susan-Lori Parks

In the Guthrie Theatre's production of *Sally & Tom* by Pulitzer Prize–winning playwright Suzan-Lori Parks, the names of Thomas Jefferson's more than six hundred slaves were displayed across a huge screen. They are named and not forgotten. Sally Hemings, the teenage slave of founding father Jefferson, reminds us through the drama's dialogue that "remembering is our power."[1] History matters.

Jefferson owned more slaves during his lifetime than any other president. Yet he worked tirelessly to establish the United States on foundations of equality and freedom. This freedom was not extended to Sally, nor to the estimated seven children she bore him; instead, Jefferson's daughter (from his marriage to his wife Martha) would free her after Jefferson's death. Did he love Sally? Did she love him? What was their authentic relationship? Jefferson was a complicated and nuanced man.

And so it is that many of our heroes lived contradictory lives: Abraham Lincoln, Benjamin Franklin, W. E. B. Du Bois, William Lloyd Garrison, and many more men of their time were compromised, flawed, and human.[2] Jefferson's immense contradictions parallel America's own convoluted national history. As Derrick Bell points out:

> The real problem of race in America is the unresolved contradiction embedded in the Constitution and never openly examined. . . . [T]his original contradiction . . . is at the heart of Black people' present day difficulty of gaining legal redress. At the heart of the Constitution was a contradiction that not all men were equal—they made a provision that the slaves were not and this would have ramification for years to come. The Constitution's biggest flaw was in protecting the institution of slavery.[3]

White Christian churches supported those contradictions despite inherent objections to them found in scriptures. This conflicted America would build hospitals, colleges and universities, and community organizations like the Boy Scouts, Girl Scouts, and the YMCA. While doing much good, white churches at the same time upheld slavery, undermined Reconstruction, and stayed silent during the civil rights movement. Today they ban books on racial history and oppose Black Lives Matter and police reform efforts.[4] Great good and great evil coexist in our present day, as they did in the eighteenth-century world of Sally and Tom.

THE PAST LIVES IN THE PRESENT

I never cared for history as a child, probably because it was a rare teacher who could make connections between my life and the history textbook. On the few occasions when it did happen, I never forgot it, and that piece of history lived on into the present. An eighth-grade social studies teacher made the civil rights movement come alive in my all-white school by creatively assigning some of us to wear tags identifying us as Black, then making sure we were treated disparagingly during the school day (an activity that probably would not be allowed today). Another teacher asked us to bring an artifact from the country our grandparents came from—in my case Czechoslovakia—thereby linking and affirming us to our ancestry. When personal experiences are understood within a broad social and historical context, it is called sociological imagination.[5]

Sociological imagination is the entanglement of race and racism in each of our lives because of America's history. A spiritual perspective sees racism as America's historical sin. As such it finds new manifestations in every generation. As sin, it has not been rooted out but allowed to fester. From the framework of CRT, it has had profound impacts on our institutions, flowing through our national religions, politics, legal system, and economy. The reasons and methods of American racism have affected our country's ability to accommodate differences of race, gender, politics, and sexual orientation. Racism and its effects are so pervasive that we cannot have a national election without racism being at the root of the process. We cannot celebrate a national sporting event without racism affecting the conduct of play. We cannot even defend against a national pandemic without racism affecting who lives and who dies. Racism is part of the social fabric, from colonization to Native American genocide, the war on Mexico, the internment of Japanese Americans, the exploitation of Puerto Rico, and the enslavement of Africans. It is a narrative of repression, economic exploration, slavery, brutal repression, and cultural neglect.[6]

For Black Americans there are two centuries of slavery: the short-lived Reconstruction, Jim Crow, the Black Codes, the KKK, lynching, segregation, mass incarceration, and disparities in housing, healthcare, mortality rates, and unequal educational opportunities. A connection can be drawn, a thread pulled through America of the past to America today. This thread runs through our policies, laws, institutions, and personal lives. To live in America is to be infected with our racial history. And a careful look at this history is necessary to understand the present and look ahead.[7]

Black History Is American History

World, American, and Black history courses exist in most social science departments. In some schools, African American studies is a separate department focusing on Black history. There may be sound reasons for these configurations, but outside of the classroom, there is one American history that embraces all Americans' stories. Black history in America is inextricably interwoven with white history, even though the latter is assumed to be "neutral" history. Two hundred years of that history is a story of slavery. The fact that America was a slaveholding society for two hundred years, and trafficked in domestic terrorism for economic gain, has effects to this day in our nation's economy, value system, psyches, and churches.

America is unique from societies that did not have slavery.[8] Race is understood and talked about differently, and its impact is particularly acute in the US as a result. Our history is an example of what white America has done, a constant reminder of what white America might do.[9] We know racial violence and hatred are possible in our society because they have already happened.

Throughout the country, especially in the slaveholding South, "the research demonstrates that the deep racial prejudice that was created by a slaveholding society is still measurably present . . . [a]nd this relationship is not just correlational but causal. . . . White people residing in the most extensive slaveholding areas in 1860 have different values around race than lower slaveholding areas: they are politically conservative and Republican, opposed to affirmative action, and score higher on scales of racial resentment."[10] Complementary research finds that the American church, especially in the South, propped up slavery, defended it from the pulpit, and at best turned a blind eye.[11] With few exceptions, the American church, whether in willful ignorance or overt racism, has historically practiced a complicit Christianity rather than a brave one.

Other historical institutional policies and processes have impacted people of color to this day: *The Indian Removal Act of 1890; the Plessey vs. Ferguson decision of 1896; the exclusion of Asian Indians from citizenship in 1923; exclusion of domestic and agricultural workers from the Social Security Act of 1935; the Wagner Act of 1935, which excluded African Americans from union membership; the Federal Housing Administration of the 1940s and 1950s; and grants to mini-mally integrated neighborhoods,* to name a few.[12]

Racial history runs through literature, architecture, music, art, and historical documents. It lives with us in the third verse of the national anthem, which includes "No refuge could save the hireling and slave" (which we never sing); the underground railroad; the preserved plantations (now sightseeing spots and prisons); and the African burial ground and slave market of pro-slavery New York City. As art historian and preservationist Fern Luskin explains her battle to preserve the Hopper-Gibbons house (a stop on the under-ground railroad):

Slavery officially ended in 1863, but the Hopper-Gibbons house is a living record of the slaves once hidden by the Abolitionists who owned it, and of the largely Irish mob who so despised their efforts to abolish slavery that they looted it and tried to burn it down. It's important that we preserve any vestiges of slavery, and the fight to end it, both for the whites who insti-tuted it and for the Black people who lived this misery.[13]

Twelve presidents owned slaves. Slave labor built the White House, the US Capitol, Georgetown University, Trinity Church, the Smith-sonian Institution, Wall Street, Fort Sumter, Harvard Law School, Monticello, and Mount Vernon. Our past, present, and future selves are implicated. American history is our common history, both Black and white. As James Baldwin said, "My history is also yours."[14] These institutional, legal, and economic structures are the terrain of CRT.

CRT AS A RESPONSE TO HISTORY

CRT argues that historical patterns of racism can be identified in our laws and institutions. Developed after the civil rights movement of the 1960s, it asked questions about why more change toward equality between races had not occurred. CRT initially examined laws and policies that reflected the legacy of slavery and segregation. Predominantly an American theory, it is applied in other contexts with variations on the theory including, for example, its application to the African continent and the impact of its colonial history on present-day Africa.

Colonization made race a social marker and practiced cultural negation in favor of Eurocentric values and cultures. This was true in the work of early missionaries, who at times negated the cultures, languages, and practices of native people groups. Missionary work is, like most enterprises, a mixed bag—doing both good and evil. The CRT concept of interest convergence, how white people benefit from policies and programs designed for Black progress, applies here and the perspective of white saviorism—that somehow good white Christians would rescue the poor indigenous people from their paganism. Although under-researched, the use of CRT as it relates to religious missions' historical and contemporary impact seems useful.

CRT is neither a rewriting of history nor a negation of traditional American history. Instead, it provides perspectives on history to tell a fuller story about how history links us to the past and lives today in both our cultural DNA and our institutions. We track the past in the present. An illustration of this phenomenon from trauma treatment is clarifying. A common trauma therapy is to talk through tragic memories, revisiting pain to open up space for forgiveness. In this way, one can move past trauma to health. Would that not be true on personal and societal levels, when it comes to racial history and America's traumatic past? Is there not a place for reflecting on, writing about, and researching the ways America's history around race is manifest in, let us say, the murder of George Floyd? How does the history of policing, school segregation, redlining, exclusionary zoning, and gentrification play out in modern-day Minneapolis? What role did the Interstate Highway Act play in destroying Black communities? How has our traumatic past affected us individually and collectively? We must revisit our pain. We must talk about it. We must try to understand it. Pain cannot have the final say.

CRT also explores legalities that create wealth gaps between Black and white people. For example, after World War II, the G.I. Bill afforded white veterans the opportunity to purchase homes and go to college, but this benefit was not extended to a million Black veterans. The G.I. Bill fostered long-term wealth for white veterans, their children, and their grandchildren. Black veterans, on the other hand, received no home loans or college benefits to build generational wealth for their children and grandchildren.[15] CRT helps us see that the problem itself was caused by previous policies and the racist assumptions embedded within them. Whether or not those lawmakers held malice in their hearts toward Black veterans does not matter. The laws themselves led to racist outcomes.

CRT invites counter-storytelling. The chronicling of our past in textbooks, academic research, and religious books has been done from a predominantly white European lens. Counter-storytelling welcomes the voices and perspectives of the marginalized, especially oppressed people of color, whose stories have traditionally been excluded. Counterstories are told by the "voices at the bottom."[16] This inclusion provides a more accurate and complete history. Sometimes there are conflicting perspectives; this is to be expected and welcomed. And yes, some of these counterstories will challenge a classic understanding of history, but all the better to get to the truth.

CRT, BACKLASH, AND SCAPEGOATING

Humans do not like to hear they are not as good as they think they are.[17] Especially the ones in power. CRT raises critical questions about American history that may be hard to accept. CRT has therefore become a scapegoat for pent-up white rage. Opposition to CRT is also a vehicle for backlash against changing racial demographics and the first Black president. America has seen this before.

Enslaved people were emancipated in 1863; the executive order issued by President Lincoln changed the legal status of more than 3.5 million enslaved African Americans. Reconstruction lasted from

1865 to 1877 and was thus described by W. E. B. Du Bois: "The slave went free; stood for a brief moment in the sun; and then moved back again toward slavery."[18] During this brief period, more than two thousand Black people were elected to public office, including two US senators and twenty-one representatives. This was a time of hope and promise for newly freed Black Americans. But it was short-lived. Major backlash to Black progress was met by the Black Codes, Jim Crow laws, lynching, and the KKK, all halting the progress of the Reconstruction years.

A similar historical pattern recurred following the progress of the 1960's civil rights movement. Hostile responses were exemplified by the assassinations of key leaders: Martin Luther King Jr., Medgar Evers, and Malcolm X; the violent bombings of Black churches; and FBI surveillance and resulting imprisonment of political prisoners and activists like Angela Davis, Fred Hampton, Huey Newton, and Susan Rosenberg. Into the 1970s, the backlash continued due to gains made by Black people in the South, anger at busing and affirmative action, and increasing economic problems, which caused poor white people to regard Black people's progress as a threat.[19] The war on drugs and Rockefeller drug laws led to the disproportionate imprisonment of men of color, commonly referred to as *mass incarceration*.

The current backlash began with the election of Barack Obama, signaling a seismic shift in the demographics of the American population. The country is rapidly becoming more ethnically and racially diverse; presently, at least one in three Americans is a person of color.[20] It is predicted that by the middle of the twenty-first century, due to immigration patterns and birthrates, white people will no longer be the majority. Rev. Bryan Massingale, a Fordham University professor and Black priest, understands the US response this way: "We are no longer a white Christian nation, and many white Christians are anxious."[21] This explains the overwhelming support of former president Donald Trump and his "Make America Great Again" slogan, which to many meant making American white again.

The changing national demographics, coupled with the election of the first Black president, first Black woman vice president, and many people of color and women reaching positions of power, work to fuel anti-Black retaliation. And CRT seems to have become the dog whistle for all things racial.

Just as the backlash to Brown v. Board of Education was fought in local public education, the current CRT pushback is fought in our nation's schools, with parents wanting to protect their children from learning true history. One result has been the demonization of CRT and laws like Florida's Stop Woke Law. This kind of racist discourse is not new, and at its core is fear. Acknowledging and altering the conditions of white supremacy, a central component of American history, makes white people uncomfortable and fearful, especially in a time of cultural shift.

Anti-racist discourse hampered and stalled school desegregation efforts by stoking fear and confusion around the NAACP's victory of Brown v. Board of Education; the 1960s was full of claims equating racial equality with communism and protests against immoral, un-American activity. We hear the same accusations against CRT this time around—a distraction to doing the real work of educational change and promotion of equity. Although many American lawmakers cannot define it, *CRT* has become a dirty term, eliciting emotional responses signaling that white children will be shamed, racial divisions will be drawn, and hate for white people will be encouraged. None of this is true, but for some, commitment to truth does not seem to matter.

THE BIG LIE

In contemporary history, the big lie refers to former president Donald Trump's denial of the 2020 election results and the subsequent attack on the US capital on January 6, 2021. But there have been earlier big lies. These include ongoing half-truths, denials, and suppression of the facts that this country was born through the crimes of genocide of Native Americans and through the slavery of African Americans. African Americans were counted as only three-fifths of a person each so that slaveholders could gain greater political representation without having to extend political rights to slaves. These lies involving the country's founding are complex, deeply rooted, and are the cause of our present trouble.[22] Then there is the lie that America is a Christian nation. As a matter of law this is wrong. The United States is a secular nation, as established in the Constitution. There were Christians among the founders, but not all were. Most belonged to churches, were baptized, attended church in varying degrees, but their intention was not to create a Christian nation.[23]

For those founders who were both Christians and slaveholders, their Bible told them stories of injustice and God's aid in freeing the slaves in Exodus 3:7–10, the historical precedence in the Bible for slave rebellion. This is why most slave masters did not want their slaves to be literate, and if they did allow them to read the Bible, they did not want them to read portions like Exodus. Black people desired literacy, but it was common to attempt to limit Bible reading among slaves out of fear that it would cause rebellion. Slave masters must have had some indirect understanding of what the Bible said, or they wouldn't have feared the slaves reading the truth.

The cognitive dissonance of following the Bible and holding slaves resulted in the creation of the original big lie that Black people were less than human, so that "all men are created equal as endowed by their creator" would not be applied to slaves. Then there were the lies purporting that the Bible supported, or at least condoned, slavery.[24] White America has been well-schooled in these lies, and according to one Black church mother, "those who believe the Bible as God's truth and Jesus as Lord and Savior must be open to discussing spiritual lies they have believed for years."[25] The truth must be told.

LEARNING AND SPEAKING THE TRUTH

So what is this truth? We are descendants of a nation of colonizers who conquered and enslaved. "The soul of America is soaked in blood and is guilty of rape—rape of this land for every available resource and rape of Black bodies on the plantation."[26] The truth is that just as the slave was property that could be bought and sold, whiteness is a commodity, a privilege that continues to buy status, employment, and economic and educational advantages. This commodity privileges white people in where they can live, what healthcare they have access to, and how they are treated by police.[27] As a result of a white supremacist society created through the economic system of slavery, there are inherent structural advantages for white people.

These advantages are even felt in the treatment of protest groups. The Southern Christian Leadership Conference, the Black Panther Party, the Weathermen, and the Black Lives Matter movement have each been labeled as domestic terrorist groups. On the other hand, when white people have participated in group lynchings, KKK gatherings, slave patrols, and neo-Nazi activities, the label has been slowly, if ever, applied.

These historic applications live on in our police departments, criminal justice systems, and policies, and can be seen in the tragedy of mass incarceration.[28] The truth is that America was built upon an ideology of racial superiority that is sinful and deadly. It is a Christian heresy.[29] Meanwhile, the church, with its fixation on individual conversion, ignores the task of transforming institutional racist policies and practices, furthering easy compromise with racism.[30] Most churches have given little thought to the gross contradictions of the Christian faith in a democracy that committed the Native American genocides and condoned slavery. Neither have they sufficiently considered the ramifications for Black and Native Americans today. It is no wonder, therefore, that CRT challenges the church at its core; it challenges the church to critically examine its faith, doctrines, history, traditions, and lies. It asks the church to acknowledge and tell the truth. But truth-telling is hard.

The truth is painful. The SBC was founded by slaveholders and held ideological and theological positions of white racial superiority. The Assemblies of God did not denounce racism as a sin until 1989, and only then with a struggle.[31] From its founding, racial separation was intentional and institutional.[32] The ELCA remains the white people's denomination.[33] The Catholic Church has been historically silent or slow to denounce police brutality and segregation. The Jesuits sold slaves to help finance Georgetown University. The Episcopal Church, in their racial justice audit of leadership, identified nine patterns of historical racism. The Church of the Nazarene was predominantly white and viewed Black people as a population to be evangelized rather than integrated; it is still highly segregated to this day.[34] And there is a history of slavery and racism within the Presbyterian church, too.[35]

For most of my adult life, I attended a Pentecostal church, hearing about the miracles of Azusa Street, and how it was the interracial beginning of the Pentecostal Church in America. This is true. William Seymour, a Black man born to former slaves in Louisiana after the Civil War, and Charles Parham, a white man born in Muscatine, Iowa, in 1873, are considered the founders of the modern Pentecostal movement that began at 312 Azusa Street in Los Angeles. Seymour met Parham at a segregated school in Texas and learned about the baptism of the Holy Spirit. Subsequently, Seymour moved to Los Angeles and led a series of revival meetings at Azusa Street from approximately 1906 to 1915, implementing what he had learned from Parham. When Parham arrived to join Seymour, he deplored the interracial mingling, and so Parham parted ways with Seymour to hold his own meetings. This racial segregation would forever influence the Assemblies of God and Church of God denominations, as well as the Pentecostal movement as a whole.[36] This is the history that I was never taught, that one of the greatest revivals and movements of the Holy Spirit in the modern day was impacted by racism.

In the service of truth, there are questions the church needs to ask: *If we were wrong about slavery, then what else are we wrong about? Where was the church historically when Black men, women, and children were lynched, castrated, and raped? What other atrocities are occurring as we continue to stand by and watch? Where was the white church during the civil rights movement? Where are we silent*

and complicit? Where does the church stand on Black Lives Matter,
mass incarceration, access to healthcare, and homelessness?

As an institution, the church has been impotent in regard to race.
The truth is that the organized church has been slow to denounce
the evils of racism. The American church follows when it should be
leading on the issue of race.[37] The truth will set you free. The CRT
backlash and scapegoating is an indication that there is resistance to
truth-telling. The effort to erase history, including CRT scholarship
and anti-racist interventions in education and government training programs (as tracked by the UCLA CRT Tracking Project), is
nothing less than the suppression of truth about race and systemic
racism. This a cultural war with CRT as the dog whistle meant to
silence truth-telling.

THE WOUND IS IN US

The backlash against and scapegoating of CRT is emblematic of the
resistance to knowing our history and acknowledging our sin. The
wounds of our history and our malignant inheritance of racism, no
matter if we are Black or white, lives in us all and will live in our
children if we do not recount it with honesty—tell our history in
all its splendors and its evils. We must include in the narrative the
sad legacy of massacres, lynching, selling bodies, slave ships, rip-
ping babies from their mothers, the Black Codes, segregation, and
the church's support and silence through the centuries. Opening
this wound is not easy, but as with any wound, unless it is cleaned
thoroughly, infection can occur. Unfortunately, because the wound
has been ignored for so long and allowed to fester, America is seriously infected.

Many still call the United States a Christian nation, but when
judging it on the lament of Jeremiah 22:13–17—"Woe to him who
builds his house by unrighteousness, and his upper rooms by
injustice. . . . Is not this to know me?"—this country falls short. And
"white America," writes Audre Lorde, "has been well-schooled in

the dehumanization of Black people."[38] Such schooling is in part responsible for the current decline of the white Christian church, leaving many with a sense of dislocation.[39] By rejecting CRT, we lose the ability to name evil. We lose a tool to identify evil as it was born in the past and lives in the present. That entails yet another loss: the opportunity to heal.

When I was a child, my mother told me there had once been a lynching in Duluth, Minnesota—an idyllic spot on Lake Superior where we vacationed. Minnesota is one of the whitest states in the country, and in June 1920, a white mob of about ten thousand people lynched three Black men—Elmer Jackson, Elias Clayton, and Isaac McGhie—who were traveling with a circus. They were accused of attacking a white couple and raping the woman, but no evidence was produced.[40] Photographs were taken of the lynchings and put on postcards to be sold. The lynching became a tourist attraction. The police stood by and directed traffic.

In 2003, Warren Read, a teacher from Washington state, did genealogical research and found that his great-grandfather had been convicted and sentenced to five years in prison for being a leader in the lynch mob. Read was so horrified that he came to Duluth for a dedication of the Clayton Jackson McGhie Memorial, and he said:

> I stand here today as a representative of my great-grandfather's legacy, and I willingly place that responsibility upon my shoulders. . . . As a family, we have used the discovery of this tool [history] for continued discovery of ourselves. This means our past, present, and future selves, and a lesson that true shame is not in the discovery of a terrible event such as this, but in the refusal to acknowledge and learn from that event.[41]

Amen and amen. And may the church acknowledge and learn from its history and the history of this country, for true shame is the refusal to acknowledge and learn from our history. As James Baldwin so eloquently said, "People are trapped in history, and history is trapped in them."[42] Even so, the scripture asks us, "Is there no balm in Gilead? Is there no physician there? Why then is there no healing for the wound of my people?" Let us be assured that there is a balm in Gilead to heal our sin-sick country.[43] Let us begin by being honest about our nation's history.

NOTES

1 *Sally & Tom,* by Suzan-Lori Parks, Guthrie Theatre, Minneapolis, Minnesota, October 20, 2022.
2 Kendi, "There Is No Debate."
3 Bell, *Faces at the Bottom.*
4 Jones, *The End of White Christian America.*
5 Mills, *The Sociological Imagination.*
6 USCC, "Brothers and Sisters to Us."
7 Lucas, *Black Priest White Church.*
8 Crenshaw, "King Was a Critical Race Theorist."
9 Bell, *And We Are Not Saved.*
10 Jones, *White Too Long.*
11 Kendi, *Stamped from the Beginning.*
12 Massingale, *Racial Justice and the Catholic Church.*
13 Luskin, personal communication.
14 Baldwin, *The Cross of Redemption.*
15 Delmont, *Half American.*
16 Matsuda, "Looking to the Bottom."
17 Chisholm, personal interview.
18 Bois and Lewis, *Black Reconstruction.*
19 Massingale, *Racial Justice and the Catholic Church.*
20 Massingale.
21 Massingale.
22 Baldwin, *The Cross of Redemption.*
23 D. L. Holmes, "The Founding Fathers."
24 Brown, *Unexpected News.*
25 John W. Kennedy, "Racism Resolution Revisited."
26 Duncan, *Dear Church.*
27 Harris, "Whiteness as Property."
28 Alexander, *The New Jim Crow.*
29 Jones, *White Too Long.*
30 Tisby and Moore, *The Color of Compromise.*
31 Kennedy, "Racism Resolution Revisited."
32 Newman, *Race and the Assemblies of God Church.*
33 Duncan, *Dear Church.*
34 Winstead, "Evangelize."

35 Yoo, *What Kind of Christianity.*
36 Newman, *Race and the Assemblies of God Church.*
37 Newman.
38 Lorde, *Sister Outsider.*
39 Jones, *The End of White Christian America.*
40 Jones, *White Too Long.*
41 Jones.
42 Baldwin, *The Cross of Redemption.*
43 Chisholm, personal interview.

CHAPTER SIX

Individual vs. Institutionalized Racism

"Racism is both overt and covert."

—Stokely Carmichael (Kwame Ture)[1]

I CAN'T BREATHE

My husband and I visited the George Floyd Memorial in October, 2021, well over a year after the murder. We expected the site on 38th and Chicago in South Minneapolis to be a compilation of grassroots tributes and, at minimum, an official government plaque acknowledging the tragic event that rocked the nation. The videotaped murder was watched millions of times on social media, played on news outlets, spawned renewed protests, and was discussed in school classrooms. For nine minutes, George Floyd pleaded for his life, arms handcuffed while Officer Derek Chauvin pressed his knee to Floyd's neck, killing him. Chauvin was convicted and found guilty on three charges—second-degree unintentional murder, third-degree murder, and second-degree manslaughter—and sentenced to twenty-two-and-a-half years' imprisonment.

Our expectations were not met. We did see and appreciate the grassroots memorial broadcast across media comprised of community murals, artwork, plastic flowers, letters, photos, and handwritten notes. As moving as these homegrown eulogies were, the absence of federal, state, or city acknowledgment of the event that shook the world was disturbing. No busts of Floyd, no municipal proclamation, no public statue, no official artifact or marker; nothing from police organizations, government agencies, organized churches, historical societies, or the larger Minnesota community to bear witness to the pain and express solidarity with the Black community. What was Minneapolis thinking? By its omission, the message was either its expression of no desire to memorialize, or a desire to make the tragedy go away—the silence of white Minnesota.

In all fairness, a permanent memorial may come. There have been ongoing talks, listening sessions, and an award of a "planning grant" in the amount of $50,000 from the National Trust for Historic Preservation, and the city put up a street sign at the location officially named George Perry Floyd Square.[2] There are mixed feelings from community members, some of whom don't want to see their neighborhood become a tourist attraction, and others who want to get back to business as usual. Yet, some want to maintain this site as a "sacred" place of remembrance. The intersection has been reopened for traffic, which businesses wanted. At the same time, others fear that not enough is being done to draw attention to racism and policing responses, especially in this area of the city. What does this debate tell us about racial justice in Minneapolis? About racial justice in America?

COLLECTIVE LAMENT AND IDENTIFICATION

The complexities of America's original sin are exemplified in this memorial debate, which points to America's need to reassess and lament its collective history around race. In American Christianity, sin tends to be limited to individual acts rather than collective sin that requires grieving, as represented in the Bible's book of Lamentations. Lamentations is seldom preached or read; it documents the fall of Jerusalem and the collective grieving of a people.[3] According to Rah, American culture tries to hide the stories of guilt and shame while extolling stories of success, thereby ignoring the pain of its victims. Public lament by a local or national community begins with identification with the oppressed. In the case of the church, it is its responsibility. By this identification it is defined. Emilio Castro, a Uruguayan minister and former general secretary of the World Council of Churches, defines this identification:

> Let the Church discover and identify itself with groups of people that suffer because of unjust situations, and who have no way of making themselves heard. The Church should be the voice of those who have no one. The Church must discover these groups and identify herself with them. Here is the modern Way of the Cross, the way of Christian responsibility.[4]

When the community identifies with the suffering and oppressed, their pain is collectively acknowledged, and public lament can be expressed. This is the work of the church, and by these actions is the church made visible. An official public memorial is one step toward the acknowledgment and collective lament of racism.

WHITE FLIGHT AND SEGREGATION

With or without the memorial, Minneapolis is infamous for the murder of George Floyd. This should not surprise anyone who grew up in Minnesota. We could have seen it coming. Growing up in a suburb of Minneapolis, Minnetonka, I did not know as a child why Minnesota was segregated, but I instinctively knew it was. Minnesota has been segregated since the second wave of the Great Migration between 1950 and 1970, when the Black population increased by 149 percent. Restrictive race-based housing covenants had prevented Black people from moving into white neighborhoods since the late 1800s, with housing discrimination continuing to be rampant well into the twenty-first century. As late as 1920, three Black men were lynched in Duluth, and Jim Crow–style legal impediments were evident in northern cities.[5] There was North Minneapolis and then the rest of Minneapolis—the urban Black core and then the white suburbs.

White flight is the historic and contemporaneous departure of white people from neighborhoods, often urban areas, when those geographical spaces become increasingly populated by people of color. This American phenomenon occurred after the Great Migration of Black Southerners to northern cities. The effect of this relocation of the white middle class and their tax base to suburban areas is the depletion of substantial funding sources and the abandonment of urban schools and neighborhoods. Years of disinvestment and neglect of the urban center then ensue.

The result is racial inequity demonstrated in disparities between white and Black people in home ownership, incarceration rates, employment, national test scores, experiences with the police.[6] Years ago I was driving from the suburbs to North Minneapolis with my six-year-old son, who grew up in the less blatantly segregated borough of Brooklyn, New York. He remarked, "Mommy, this is so different from where auntie lives." His aunt lived in an all-white affluent suburban neighborhood. Only six years old, and the disparity was evident to him.

According to Myers, the director of the Roy Wilkins Center for Human Relations and Social Justice at the University of Minnesota, this is "the Minnesota paradox": Most Minnesotans are concerned about what is happening in their state but have trouble attributing the inequity to institutional racism and systemic causes. And many cannot fathom how they or their relatives before them might be actively or tacitly complicit. White flight is just one example of such complicity.

WHITE FLIGHT AND THE CHURCH

The white church fled as well. During the second half of the twentieth century in America, white Protestants fled from the cities to the suburbs. According to Soong-Chan Rah, an associate professor at North Park Theological Seminary in Chicago, white Christians thought of cities as evil places of sin and hostility, and so fled to the safety of the suburbs from non-white and non-Protestants newcomers.[7] After World War II, there was an intentional abandonment of urban areas by white people during the church growth movement and the previous Great Migration from the South, when Black people fled domestic terrorism, rural areas with unemployment and underemployment, and some poverty-populated cities.[8] White people exchanged commitments to neighborhoods and community for a mall mentality of church, shopping convenience, and homogeneity. The city was deemed dangerous, with government financing and policies making it possible for white flight.[9]

This church flight was most prevalent from the 1950s through the 1970s, resulting in the residential and church segregation that persists to the present. It was institutionally sanctioned by the church, as exemplified in Mulder's 2012 case study of the Christian Reformed Church in North America. Mulder's research concludes that the white flight of churches and families from Chicago was supported by congregational polices, social church networks, and administrative systems that made white flight relatively easy.[10] After the church abandoned American cities, the white suburbs were viewed as the new Jerusalem.

THE SUBURBS AND THE CITY

After visiting the George Floyd Memorial, my husband and I spent a day in one of these suburbs, Minnetonka. I grew up in this school district. My father was a middle-class laborer, but my parents bought a home in this upper-class community—a community that would not have been open to Black people. I attended school in one of the highest-ranking districts in the state, where a significant portion of school funding is based on property taxes. Hence the common phenomenon of young parents checking out the school districts for funding, racial composition, and test scores before buying homes. While there, I received a distinguished alumna award for my work and scholarship at a special awards breakfast. We also participated in homecoming weekend, where we rode on the alumni float through the streets of the town and attended the homecoming football game. It was an honor, and it was lovely. It was also illuminating.

This school district is predominantly upper- and middle-class, boasting a 96 percent graduation rate, with test scores in the top 20 percent of the state. The district is 85 percent white, and 15 percent Asian and Hispanic, with statistics for the Black population unclear. Just 5 percent of students are eligible for free lunch.[11] Compare this to Edison High School in North Minneapolis, a school where 83 percent of students are people of color and 17 percent are white. The graduation rate is 76 percent; test scores are in the bottom 50 percent of the state, and 72 percent of students are eligible for free lunch (an indicator of household income near or below the federal poverty line). These statistics indicate that the different opportunities afforded to white and Black children are related to segregation. Both qualitative and quantitative research support this explanation.[12] Those opportunities are institutionalized in school resources and facilities. Access to quality healthcare, housing options, employment, and economic opportunities impacts children's lives in and out of school. Black children have disproportionately less access to those opportunities than white children in the suburbs. The inequities between Minnetonka and Edison can be replicated with dozens of comparisons between suburban white schools and urban Black schools. Location and segregation matter.

Racial segregation by school districts often correlates with rates of poverty, inadequate healthcare, lower life expectancy, income-related health disparities, higher infant and mother mortality rates, obesity, lack of access to fresh fruits and vegetables, sparse mental health resources, and inadequate drug treatment options.[13] A CRT-informed analysis explains the facts in front of us. Simplistic appeals to personal responsibility do not.

COVID AND RACISM

People of color are more likely to have preexisting health conditions, making them more susceptible to contracting Covid-19 and more likely to be hospitalized because of the virus. Nationwide,

INDIVIDUAL VS. INSTITUTIONALIZED RACISM

Black people died at 2.4 times the rate of white people. Substandard healthcare before, during, and after the pandemic created race-based disparities in our healthcare system. Dr. William F. Marshall from the Mayo Clinic further explains:

> Research increasingly shows that racial and ethnic minorities are disproportionately affected by coronavirus disease 2019 (COVID-19) in the United States. . . . COVID-19 hospitalization rates among non-Hispanic Black people and Hispanic or Latino people were both about 4.7 times the rate of non-Hispanic white people. While there's no evidence that people of color have genetic or other biological factors that make them more likely to be affected by COVID-19, they are more likely to have underlying health conditions. . . . But experts also know that where people live and work affects their health. Over time, these factors lead to different health risks among racial and ethnic minority groups.[14]

Covid is a recent example of what the CRT framework so effectively identifies—institutional, structural, systemic racism. These terms are synonymous, and throughout this book are used interchangeably. CRT frames racism not in individual acts, but in the trends and policies that have systemically created Covid inequity: substandard healthcare, poor or no health insurance, inadequate nutritional options, necessity to work during the pandemic, preexisting medical conditions, and generations of economic and demographic inequity disproportionally impacting urban neighborhoods.

According to the Brookings Institute, segregation is persistent even while we are becoming ethnically and racially diverse as a nation.[15] Federally subsidized suburbs created generational wealth for the white flighters, but were designed to exclude Black people. Redlining and reverse redlining are structural practices of the real estate finance industry that have excluded Black people from both home ownership and home ownership loans. Recently, subprime loan fraud targeted Black people and Latinos. Decades of predatory lending practices constitutes institutional racism.

The CRT framework examines policies and practices of under-investment in Black communities, businesses, and homeowners, over-policing of minority neighborhoods, and devaluation of residential property owned by minorities. These policies result in substandard schools, subpar healthcare exacerbating Covid-19 contraction, less access to capital for Black entrepreneurs, proportionally higher incarceration rates for people of color, lowered public safety, and segregated places of worship.

CHRISTIANITY AND RACISM

Why should this matter to the church? The Christian church is bound by the scriptures and from lessons learned from the life of Christ to love our neighbor as ourselves, with a special emphasis on the poor and oppressed among us (Psalms 10:1 and 72:12). Throughout scripture, and particularly in the New Testament (Luke 6:20), this mission is consistently demonstrated. According to Karl Barth, the renowned Swiss theologian: "Man is made responsible to all those who are poor and wretched in his eyes, that he is summoned on his part to espouse the cause of those who suffer wrong. Why? Because in them it is manifested to him what he himself is in the sight of God."[16] According to Barth, because we are poor and oppressed in God's eyes, our affinity with the oppressed and poor of the earth is in character with God, and God always takes a stand on behalf of the oppressed.[17] Dietrich Bonhoeffer, the martyred German theologian who stood up to the Nazi regime, concurs, adding that Christians have a moral and ethical responsibility to stand up to evil systems. This is costly grace.[18] James H. Cone, the founder of Black theology, agreed with both Barth and Bonhoeffer, and applied this prefer-ence to the poor and oppressed to Black people in America.[19] Cone makes the case that Old Testament prophets Amos, Hosea, Isaiah, and Micah concerned themselves with social justice, and Jesus in the

Christian Bible gives preference to the poor and oppressed.[20] Howard Thurman, the distinguished scholar-teacher, author, theologian, and civil rights leader put it this way:

> The basic fact is that Christianity as it was born in the mind of this Jewish teacher and thinker [Jesus] appears as a technique of survival for the oppressed. That it became, through the intervening years, a religion of the powerful and the dominant, used sometimes as an instrument of oppression, must not tempt us into believing that it was thus in the mind and life of Jesus.[21]

Were Jesus to be in the flesh now, his concerns would arguably include systemic racism as lived out in our segregated schools, neighborhoods, and places of worship. Churches and Christians are complicit in segregation through white flight, voting patterns, and personal choice. Physical segregation by race intersects with class and social segregation. Most white Americans (91 percent) have social networks that are nearly all white, while Black and Latino Americans have more diverse social networks.[22] These class- and race-based social networks provide the economics to support better schools, hospitals, and larger, more affluent churches.

In theory, the church ought to be the least segregated collective body as "the salt of the earth"; instead, the American church has become one of the most racially segregated institutions.[23] Unfortunately the familiar phrase "Sunday morning is the most segregated hour of the week" is true. Indeed, there are trends in the church echoing back to colonialism, and missions identified as incarnational ministry, urban missions, mission trips, and justice work, some superficial while other efforts are true long-term allegiances and ministries for racial justice. But in general, the American church is divided by race, and ministry is paternalistic and short-term. Interracial churches do exist, often with white lead pastors, yet most Americans still live in racially segregated neighborhoods, have mostly same-race relationships, and attend same-race churches.[24]

KINGDOMS OF DARKNESS AND
CRITICAL RACE THEORY

Drawing from Walter Wink's extensive research on power in the Bible, "the language of power pervades the whole New Testament," and the powers are both "heavenly and earthly, divine and human, spiritual and political, invisible and structural."[25] In this regard, the familiar Ephesians 6:12, "For we do not wrestle against flesh and blood, but against the rulers, against the authorities, against the cosmic powers over this present darkness, against the spiritual forces of evil in the heavenly places," is interpreted to reference political, economic, and like systems in modern terms.[26]

CRT aligns closely to Ephesians 6:12. The contemporaneous actualization of Paul's words parallel the core idea that both sin and racism go beyond individual people but are instead embedded in systems or kingdoms of darkness. These systems are mostly invisible yet powerful, and they work against the kingdom of God.[27] Following this line of reasoning, racism is not just the result of bias or prejudice but present in larger structures of oppression—harder to identify, and more insidious as a power of darkness.

St. Paul wrote about "principalities and powers," and CRT scholars write of social constructs and structural bias. Paul says the struggle is not one of individual people's "flesh and blood," but larger "principalities and powers," or structures of influence.

Some Christians fear that, if we focus on racism as a collective sin, we will negate individual responsibility, or personal salvation. Not so. Personal responsibility and individual acts of sin will always need to be addressed. Journalist Darrell Lackey frames it this way:

> Many evangelical/fundamentalists seem to think if we teach or give credence to CRT, we are somehow taking away the focus of the Gospel regarding salvation and the idea of our individual fallenness. I think each fear is based on a misunderstanding of scripture and Christian theology. First, the good news of salvation (the Gospel) is not simply about the individual salvation

of people or souls; it's about the salvation and redemption of the entire cosmos. The entire cosmos died with Jesus upon the cross and he brought the entire cosmos out of the grave in his resurrection. Second, while we need to keep in mind individual choices and decisions, we also need to remember that those never happen in a vacuum. It is impossible to understand the root causes of many crimes without considering poverty, child abuse, and other factors. We can hold people accountable individually for their decisions, while at the same time addressing the larger forces at work that contributed to the choices available to them and their decision making.[28]

CRT AND THE BIBLE

There is widespread agreement that the scriptures cannot be understood without historical context. In that regard, Jesus was part of an oppressed minority group. He was a Jew born into a colonized environment under the Roman Empire. He lived a poor agrarian existence. This context and perspective guide His words and actions.

Although not normally applied to the study of the scriptures, CRT's focus on systems and institutions of oppression are instructive. It examines ancient systems that impacted biblical history, applying the analysis to current American contexts and contemporary systems. CRT's lens can help us avoid tragic, literal, and abusive readings of the Bible that support American slavery and white supremacy.[29] There is little dispute about misguided interpretations of the Bible used to justify the slave trade, Jim Crow, segregated worship, opposition to interracial marriage, and the like.[30] CRT is one tool to expose, examine, and research both historical and contemporary systems of oppression. As a theoretical framework, it can provide insight and perspective on the application of Ephesians 6:12 and the Gospels to a twenty-first-century church. The collective sin of racism in the American churches through its abandoning of the city, its history of segregation by choice, white flight, and continued unwillingness to take responsibility for complicity is unfortunate. CRT helps us to see this. Despite social progress, increased mobility, and increasingly diverse racial demographics, inequity remains. CRT helps us understand this inequity, and the church could benefit from applying a CRT lens to its reading of the Bible. Racism need not be permanent should society and the church resolve to decry it and then determine to change.

"BUT I AM NOT RACIST"

The distinction between individual and systemic racism is important. White people often say, "But I am not a racist," and in terms of individual acts of racism, most white people are not. As this chapter has laid out, the problem lies in the seemingly invisible systems and institutional racism that are harder to pinpoint than racist words, microaggressions, and acts. The invisible nature of systemic racism is harder to detect than blatant acts of individual racism

This chapter opened with my visit to site of the George Floyd Memorial and the greater Minneapolis area a year after Floyd's murder. This was where an act of individual racism by one bad police officer occurred. CRT is a tool for unmasking the systemic racism within the Minneapolis Police Department, which harkens back to the origins of slave codes and slave patrols in New England. The ways police departments operate are a prime example of systemic racism. The disparities between the two Minneapolis school districts, one suburban and one urban, further highlight systemic racism. This type of racism is harder to identify and seemingly invisible. It's especially difficult to see systemic racism as it relates to the church. The illusive nature of systemic racism connects to the scripture from Ephesians 6:12. Related to the sin of collective racism, this verse indicates that there are institutional authorities and forces (policies, systems, governing bodies, historical precedent, etc.) that are barriers and in opposition to the Gospel. Understood this way, the obligation of the church is to recognize these systems and work through prayer and action in addressing them.

This is the concept of being "woke" to these larger kingdoms of darkness. In adult learning, being woke is called a disorienting dilemma that propels transformation. The disorienting dilemma for a person of faith is reconciling racist systems in America with an informed biblical understanding of powers of darkness and determining God's will within that understanding. That was Bonhoeffer's dilemma, King's dilemma, Desmond Tutu's dilemma, and ultimately Christ's dilemma. This is a healthy revelation. An accurate understanding of CRT can assist white people both in comprehending the collective sin of systemic racism in America and in assessing their own personal responsibility.

The next chapter examines individual and collective obstacles in admitting complicity, being anti-racist, and becoming allies. Chapter 7 opens with an example of white fragility—white people's defensive stance to claims of an America and a church steeped in white supremacy and privilege.

NOTES

1 Carmichael and Hamilton, *Black Power: The Politics of Liberation.*
2 Hooten, "Minneapolis to Install Permanent Monument."
3 Rah and McNeil, *Prophetic Lament.*
4 Cone, *Black Theology & Black Power.*
5 Burnside, "African Americans in Minnesota."
6 Ellis, "Minneapolis Had This Coming."
7 Rohr, *Immortal Diamond.*
8 Rah and McNeil, *Prophetic Lament.*
9 Seligman, *Block by Block.*
10 Mulder, "Nuances of White Flight."
11 "Minnetonka Senior High School."
12 Lleras, "Race, Racial Concentration, and the Dynamics."
13 "Health, Income, Poverty."
14 Sparks, "Coronavirus Infection by Race."
15 Hadden Loh, Coes, and Buthe, "Separate and Unequal."
16 Barth, *The Doctrine of God.*
17 Barth.

18 Bonhoeffer, *The Cost of Discipleship.*
19 Cone, *Black Theology & Black Power.*
20 Cone, *A Black Theology of Liberation.*
21 Thurman and Harding, *Jesus and the Disinherited.*
22 Cole, "Understanding Segregation Today."
23 Emerson and Smith, *Divided by Faith.*
24 Emerson and Smith.
25 Wink, *Naming the Powers.*
26 Sharp, "Voices"; Wink.
27 Sharp, "Voices."
28 Lackey, "In Light of Ephesians."
29 Kendi, *Stamped.*
30 Kendi.

CHAPTER SEVEN

White Supremacy, Privilege, and Fragility

"It's time for white Christians to be more Christian than white—
which is necessary to make racial reconciliation and healing possible."
—Jim Wallis

DEFINITIONAL THEFT

During the historic Ketanji Brown Jackson Supreme Court hearings, Texas senator Ted Cruz held up and disparaged textbooks that I use when teaching CRT to graduate students at John Jay College of Criminal Justice. I should not have been surprised. Conservative politicians, religious leaders, schoolboards, and parents continue to malign diversity education and commit definitional theft regarding CRT. Patricia Williams, a CRT legal scholar, defines the compilation of misinterpreted, distorted, and bogus claims about CRT as "stealing."[1] Whether motivated by ignorance or malice, anti-CRT education policies, book bans, restrictions on teaching, and divisive rhetoric are rampant. It's fraud, and it's our children who will be swindled.

TEACHING CRT

I've been teaching CRT for over twenty years to graduate and undergraduate students. As a white female humanities professor, I see assaults on CRT as attacks on academic freedom, but even more so a missed opportunity for our students to understand the unique and powerful force that race has been in America. CRT is a tool for my students to engage in conversations about their own racial identities, and a framework for them to engage in long overdue discussions about race and its impact on all of us.

I teach in racially and ethnically diverse classrooms, and I can tell you our students are grappling to comprehend race in America. Some are fearful of talking about race, and others seek language and perspectives to make sense of the racial dynamics that keep rearing their heads. The classroom has featured discussions about policing practices, redlining, school segregation, gentrification, voter suppression, and substandard healthcare during the Covid-19 epidemic, all of which highlight racial disparities.

My students born outside the United States are often confused by America's brand of racism. CRT provides the jargon to make a distinction between individual acts of racism or "one bad apple," and systemic, historical racism. Learning an inclusive history of America, which decenters white historical narratives and includes the counterstories of Black people, offers them greater clarity and accuracy. CRT is a lens into the past's presence in current American institutions: criminal justice, housing, healthcare, and education.

BENEFITS TO WHITE STUDENTS

My white students benefit the most from learning CRT. They need the conceptual learning that CRT provides to better understand white supremacy and gain a deeper, broader perspective of race. Contrary to claims that learning this theory will make white people feel shame or guilt, my own experience and that shared by my students is relief and increasing comfort with conversations around race. Astute students understand their privilege and comprehend that with privilege comes responsibility. And truth be told, we may all benefit from a healthy amount of guilt about American history as it regards race.

Guilt is different from shame. Guilt can be positive and motivate transformation; shame is debilitating and self-destructive.[2]

I teach a course called Communication Theory and include CRT as one of many well-established interdisciplinary theories. When teaching *Nonverbal Communication*, I use CRT to define race as a social and nonverbal construct, not a biological one. We examine nonverbal evidence of racism in our neighborhoods, prisons, and architecture, reflecting on the development of our perceptions based on nonverbal racial cues when interacting with others. In my course on *Race, Prisons, and Punishment*, CRT provides an invaluable historical lens from which to understand mass incarceration, the war on drugs, and the origins of policing. This is what good theories do—provide a lens with which to see our world. Is it the only lens? No. But it is an important one for this moment. CRT is a good, timely theory.

NORMALIZATION OF WHITENESS

CRT also helps us understand how American churches have become hyper-segregated and white-centric.[3] *White-centric* means that white culture is normalized; white culture is the baseline in society and churches. How does this normalization of whiteness work? An example related to the church comes from Daniel Hill's book *White Awake*. Hill's seminary professor illustrated the normalization of whiteness in an educational setting:

> There are required classes that are just called theology [in seminary]. But when you go to the electives, you will see that, in the spirit of diversity, we offer an array of additional theology classes: Black theology, Latin theology, Asian theology, etc. A question begs to be asked: Why do all of those theology classes have a modifier before them? Where is the category of white theology?[4]

Whiteness as a racial concept is socially constructed and normalized as the racial identity to which others are compared. Racial minorities are contrasted with whiteness as a standard or default position. In the words of Toni Morrison, "In this country, American means white. Everybody else has to hyphenate."[5] White American is the baseline from which other races are referenced. Because of this normalization of white culture, people of color are seen as the other.

In the white evangelical church, which is a reflection of larger white society, whiteness is the criteria by which all other races are compared. Tranby and Hartmann explain this normalization of whiteness:

> Attitudes of evangelicals are deeply structured by and consonant with dominant America ideologies. For evangelicals, social norms, values, structures, institutions and the religio-cultural toolkit are intimately bundled up with ideas of race and nation. Because the norms and values that form the evangelical idea of "American-ness" are implicitly white, the demands for increased recognition for minority groups is perceived as a threat to these values and norms.[6]

White people then view people of color as problems to be fixed. This perspective has frequently manifested in suburban white churches doing paternalistic urban ministry to those "poor people in the inner city"—short-term charity. CRT is a threat to this ministry approach because it challenges a white norm that solely addresses individuality, working hard to get ahead, and tropes of personal responsibility. American Christians hold strong opposition to the notion that "social outcomes could be determined by any forces other than merit, effort, and hard work of individuals themselves."[7]

As previously stated, critics of CRT assert that the theory's centering of systemic racism promotes a worldview of victimization of people of color. They claim that attributing racism to systemic causes creates long-term dependency and victim mentality rather than responsibility and self-empowerment. They purport that CRT is detrimental to persons of color and inadvertently harms them.[8]

However, understanding the framework of CRT does not negate or eliminate personal responsibility. Taking responsibility for actions is what makes us human. However, CRT reminds us of the context and histories in which choices, opportunities, and possible courses of action are influenced and limited.[9] America is an individualist society where personal accountability is held in high regard, and nowhere is this more evident than in the Christian church. When it negates the larger collective forces that impact an individual's ability to freely and equally exercise that responsibility, however, this perspective is problematic. It is not an *either-or* proposition; it is a *both-and* one.

The normalization of whiteness is invisible to many white people. The white race is centralized, and therefore, most white people do not experience the struggle and marginalization of other races.[10] It is not uncommon for white people to not identify as white, or to not think much about their race at all. Whiteness is the default and, as such, brings with it socioeconomic privileges born of white supremacy.

WHITE SUPREMACY

White supremacy is not limited to white militants in Charlottesville, Virginia carrying Confederate flags and spewing racist language. It is not even a belief that white people are superior to those of other races, although it does include these. White supremacy conjures pictures of the KKK in hoods, screaming racial slurs and burning crosses. But, as academic Eddie Glaude Jr. argues, white supremacy is much more. It determines who is valued in society and how society organizes itself, casting some people higher than others. It is practices and policies guided by a belief that white people are more valuable than others.[11]

White supremacy involves the systems, institutions, laws, and norms that support the dominance of the white race. This prioritizing of the white race can be conscious or unconscious and often feels invisible. White supremacy in the American church has a long history and often intersects with other types of discrimination. And because it is characteristic of systems and institutions, white supremacy is a phenomenon aptly explained through the tools of CRT.

According to Robert Jones, the root cause of white supremacy in America is the institution of slavery, of which white American Christianity was complicit.[12] In the eighteenth and nineteenth centuries, after the removal of Native Americans from their land, Protestant churches were made up of slaveholding members. These included Baptists, Episcopalians, and Catholics. Segregation of churches by race was the rule, and its impact is present to this day. Jones writes, "White Christian institutions and people were the primary architects and guardians of this exclusionary form of Americanism [white supremacy] which made full membership in the nation contingent on skin tone and religious belief."[13] Because the white Christian church and its members historically supported slavery and undermined Reconstruction, the influence and partnership of white supremacy and large swathes of the organized white church in America continues to this day.

WHITE PRIVILEGE

An understanding of white supremacy sets the context to acknowledge another recently battered around term—*white privilege*. One of the first to name white privilege was Peggy McIntosh, an American feminist, anti-racism activist, and scholar. In her now famous 1989 essay "White Privilege: Unpacking the Invisible Knapsack," she outlined the ways in which she experienced unfair advantages because of being white:

I began to count the ways in which I enjoy unearned skin privilege and have been conditioned into oblivion about its existence. My schooling gave me no training in seeing myself as an oppressor, as an unfairly advantaged person, or as a participant in a damaged culture. I was taught to see myself as an individual whose moral state depended on her individual moral will. My schooling followed the pattern my colleague Elizabeth Minnich has pointed out: White people are taught to think of their lives as morally neutral, normative, and average, and also ideal, so that when we work to benefit others, this is seen as work which will allow "them" to be more like "us."[14]

Whiteness is a racialized commodity of advantage that is exchanged for social benefits and access to "better" housing, healthcare, education, employment, mobility, criminal justice, et cetera.[15] With the possession of whiteness, white people enjoy benefits and access to safer neighborhoods, better-resourced schools and hospitals, as well as legal and police protections. On a personal level, the privilege to shop at any store in any neighborhood and not be followed or watched is a birthright of whiteness.

Translated to my own multiracial megachurch experience with a white pastor, I can count the ways I enjoyed unearned skin privilege with greater access to the white leadership, opportunities for ministry, books authored by people who look like me, and an assurance that I could voice my disagreement and be heard. I assumed that I would be taken seriously. There was one instance among many that tested this assumption. The church was hierarchical in its governance, with no board of directors except the pastor and his family. There was no structural vehicle by which members, the majority people of color, could voice their ideas, opinions, and questions. There was no budget transparency and no access to a strategic plan. But questions were asked, murmurings occurred, discontent and confusion were expressed. I assumed we could organize and form an advisory board of members to express concerns to the white pastor. My white privilege taught me that I had this right. However, for many of my Black and brown church friends, this was not their assumption. Many expressed their fear, hesitancy, and confusion as to their right to question the pastor as the man of God. My privilege taught me to assume I have this right and can exercise it.

My church taught colorblindness. It gave me no window through which to see myself as an oppressor, as an advantaged church member, or as someone in need of repentance because of the sin of racism in and outside the church. I was taught to see myself as a colorblind person responsible only for my individual sins. My church taught me to think of myself as spiritually and culturally superior because of my choice to follow Christ the American way and to work toward evangelizing others, especially poor people and people of color, so they could have a church experience like mine.

It was not uncommon for white churches from across the country to visit our inner-city congregation to do short-term missions to help the poor urban residents, then to go back home and give testimonies about their experiences. Some Sundays were like museum days, where groups (culturally insensitively dressed) from suburban white churches came to tour this urban church as if they were visiting some sort of museum display. Most groups were from white suburban churches, and they enjoyed the multiracial choir, gospel music, and charismatic worship. Sometimes they spent several days at the church's adult learning center, tutoring the students for a couple of hours. The groups then returned to suburbia, seemingly satisfied that they had completed "missions."

White privilege is the everyday invisible social and economic upper hand. Acceptance of this edge in life can be hard because it places our self-worth, achievement, and concept of ourselves in question. To question our achievements in light of advantage requires humility. White pastors can have difficulty with owning up to their privilege, both in being white and in being male. It takes courage to accept that you have a leg up. And as stated previously but bears repeating—with privilege comes responsibility. How will you work to make change within yourself and your church? How will you listen to the voices of others? Hill states that in this process of questioning, white people are quasi-victims by not having struggled with marginalization and oppression; therefore, there is "little stamina for race-based stress."[16] This debility is called *white fragility*.

WHITE FRAGILITY

White fragility is not a term or tenet of CRT, but a CRT framework can alleviate or address it. White fragility is a defensive stance adopted in response to the challenges of white supremacy, white privilege, and conversations around race. It refers to individual, rather than systemic, behavior. Robin DiAngelo coined the term "white fragility" to describe the disbelieving defensiveness that white people exhibit when their ideas about race and racism are confronted—and when they feel implicated in white supremacy. It is individual white people insisting that they are not racist, they have Black friends, or they are not part of the problem.

It is a space of denial. Perhaps the unreasoned response of anger and fear to CRT includes a fair amount of white fragility. Also contributing is the American individualist culture, which is highly racialized, blind to white supremacy, and prone to fragility when challenged with white complicity.[17] When first reading *White Fragility*, I felt the examples rang true. I saw myself, my white friends, and family in some of the defensiveness. The erasure and dismissiveness are particularly egregious. When broaching the subject of race and racism, white people frequently dismiss it with, "Get over it already," or "The past is the past; we've made a lot of progress." Another common response is, "You are always talking about race—you are an old hippie." But perhaps the strongest negation of racial conversations is manifested in silence.

THE SILENCE OF THE WHITE CHURCH

In 1963, Martin Luther King Jr. responded to the silence of the white church in his "Letter from a Birmingham Jail":

> I have looked at the South's beautiful churches with their lofty spires pointing heavenward. I have beheld the impressive outlines of her massive religious education buildings. Over and

over, I have found myself asking: "What kind of people worship here?" Who is their God? . . . Where are their voices of support when bruised and weary Negro men and women decided to rise from the dark dungeons of complacency to the bright hills of creative protest?

The letter was written in response to eight white clergy who did not argue with the goals of the civil rights protests but instead the timing. Their fears seemed to be of more bloodshed, and they advocated for a gradualist approach.[18] King's letter questions and disputes the silence of the white church during the civil rights movement.

The same questions could be asked during the protests that occurred after the murder of George Floyd and so many others, including the victims of the shootings in Buffalo and Charleston. The white church is silent during protests, and little is said from the pulpit. Yes, there have been exceptions, but the majority of white people and white churches are silent, and silence can be worse than opposition. Straightforward argument, at the very least, offers active engagement.

Silence signals disengagement likened to the silent treatment in a relationship. When demands are made upon individuals to engage in conflict—in this case, engage in conversations around race—there is withdrawal. This pattern of demand and withdrawal is a manifestation of white fragility. Requests to address racism are met by avoidance through silence. How many times have you heard sermons on racial sin from the pulpit? How many times have you attended a Bible study that looked at Jesus's resistance to ethnic and racial hatred and systems of oppressive power? As in relationships, this kind of silence does extensive damage.

SPIRITUAL AWAKENING—WOKE

A spiritual awakening is a transformative experience that expands a person's sense of self to embrace an eternal and wider truth—thus being born again to Christ, salvation, stirring in the Spirit, quaking. Other terms for this way of knowing include *renewal, being raised, resurrection,* and being *woke*. It alerts one to larger realities, whether they be deity, spirituality, or justice. All involve a new way of seeing and knowing. These subjective experiences change our cognitive schemata to understand the world and our relation to it differently. This is the essence of accepting Christ, good news, or the Gospel: an opening up to God and a transformation of the self to encompass a larger truth.

The word *woke* and the phrase *stay woke* are not new. They were developed by African Americans in the 1930s and became part of Black vernacular, signifying awareness of racial, political, and social justice. The earliest use of *stay woke* was from the African American blues musician, Lead Belly, in 1938, in the song "Scottsboro Boys," about nine Black teenage boys accused of raping two white women. Following a rendition of the song, the musician spoke about meeting the Scottsboro boys and the state of racism in Alabama. He cautioned his Black audience to be vigilant to the dangers in cities, streets, and rural areas of America.

This expression reemerged after the shooting of Michael Brown in Ferguson, Missouri in 2014 and was used by Black Lives Matters protesters to draw awareness to police brutality and misconduct. Through its internet proliferation, the term was adopted by white people to represent their support for Black Lives Matter. Its use has spread internationally and was added to the *Oxford English Dictionary* and *Meriam-Webster* in 2017. Some criticize its use by white people as cultural appropriation.

I pose a variant perspective on *stay woke* from the Bible. The scripture tells us to be aware of and attentive to evil: "Be alert and of sober mind. Your enemy the devil prowls around like a roaring lion looking for someone to devour"; "Wake up, and strengthen the things that remain, which were about to die; for I have not found your deeds completed in the sight of my God."[19] There are over forty-five references to wakening, woke, arising, and being alert in both the Old and New Testaments. Rather than being a disparaging phrase, "staying woke" is a deeply spiritual notion implying an alertness to evil—a deeply Christian concept. The words of Barbara Lee, twelve-term congresswoman from the 13th District of California, apply:

> But we will only succeed if we reject the growing pressure to retreat into cynicism and hopelessness. . . . We have a moral obligation to "stay woke," take a stand and be active; challenging injustices and racism in our communities and fighting hatred and discrimination wherever it rises.[20]

REFLECTION AND REPENTANCE

Chicago pastor and author Daniel Hill writes, prays, and talks about repentance when addressing what he calls the sin of white supremacy and racism. He writes:

> I regularly and comfortably repent for the sins of white Christians—both for mine and for the sins of my community. It isn't because I think I'm better than everybody else or that I'm trying to prove that some bad white Christians out there need to be chastised. No, I repent all the time because I believe I'm surrounded by the sickness of racism.[21]

I am comfortable with this perspective, although I do not frame my understanding as an anti-racist in terms of repentance. But it makes sense both on an individual and collective level. Like all types of sins, racism is insidious, infectious, often hidden, and persistent. Repentance and lament seem appropriate responses.

Jones takes a different approach. He proposes that churches can start the process of being woke with reflection, then asking questions like the following: (1) How do the church and church grounds physically embody whiteness in its stained glass windows, paintings, signs, and advertisements? (2) Do the church website and social media sites reflect white as the norm? (3) Are children's educational materials telling a diverse story? How many 1950s-era materials depicting only white people are still around? (4) How do we tell our own church histories? How honest are we in our complicity with racism? (5) How do hymns and worship songs associate white with purity and black with sin and evil? Powerful but subtle racism often is below the level of consciousness. (6) Does the preaching address the sin of white supremacy? Is widespread silence from the pulpit about race and racism your church's experience? (7) Does the church budget reflect a commitment to racial justice and reparations? (8) In what ways does your white congregation make a commitment to supporting a Black or multiracial church or parachurch organization that serves Black or multiracial community members? Good questions and a beginning.[22]

In terms of CRT, there is no call to repentance, no hatred of white people, and no shaming of white people. CRT as an activist theory promotes awareness—wokeness—to expose systems of oppression based on white supremacy. Arguably, progress has occurred since the civil rights movement. Nonetheless, the work of racial justice is not done. CRT is one theory that enlightens our way. This chapter opened with teaching CRT in college classrooms and its benefits for white students. Teaching and embracing CRT in the church can be a powerful tool to problematize the individualistic mindset so pervasive in American Christianity. Just as large segments of the church in America have galvanized around pro-abortion initiatives, a galvanization around the dismantling of white supremacy would be nothing but revolutionary.

In the words of President Biden when visiting grieving families after the racist massacre in Buffalo, "White supremacy is a poison." And so it is: potent, invisible, and rampant, infecting us all.

NOTES

1 Cobb and Guariglia, *Kerner Commission Report.*
2 Brown, *Critical Race Theory.*
3 Emerson and Smith, *Divided by Faith.*

4 Hill and McNeil, *White Awake.*
5 Hoby, "Toni Morrison."
6 Tranby and Hartmann, "Critical Whiteness Theories."
7 Brown, *Daring Greatly.*
8 Walker, "New White Supremacy."
9 Schwartz and Chaney, *Gifts from the Dark.*
10 Tranby and Hartmann, "Critical Whiteness Theories."
11 Glaude, *Democracy in Black.*
12 Jones, *White Too Long.*
13 Jones.
14 McIntosh, "White Privilege."
15 Harris, "Whiteness as Property."
16 Hill and McNeil, *White Awake.*
17 Robin DiAngelo, *White Fragility.*
18 Bass, Cobb, and Harvey, *Blessed Are the Peacemakers.*
19 1 Pt 5:8-9; Rom 3:11; Rv 3:2 (NIV).
20 Lee, "Congresswoman Barbara Lee."
21 Hill and McNeil, *White Awake.*
22 Jones, *White Too Long.*

CHAPTER EIGHT

Counter-Storytelling and the Subversive Jesus

"He taught them many things by parables."

—Mark 4:2 NIV

My nephew, an accomplished American roots musician, recently visited Tulsa, Oklahoma and The Church Studio established by musician, songwriter, and producer Leon Russell, whose life-sized bronze statue stands out front. As my nephew tells it, Tulsa is a magical and historical place. Tulsa's Church Studio was established in 1972. Its website reports that the original church (before it was a studio) survived the race riots of 1921. Those race riots could be more accurately described as white domestic terrorism. On May 31 and June 1, 1921, mobs of white residents burned to the ground the wealthy Black Tulsa district of Greenwood. Gangs of white men armed by public officials set fire to banks, businesses, the hospital, and the library. Hundreds of mostly Black Tulsa residents were killed, and thousands left homeless. It is one of the worst incidents of racial violence in US history, one that for years was covered up.

My nephew is a historian, and he knows this history, but most Americans did not until recently. This genocide is a counterstory kept alive by survivors and ancestors—a hidden and shameful narrative. Tulsa is both The Church Studio and Black Wall Street—music capital and racial tragedy. But the history that is told depends on who is doing the telling.

The dominant Black Wall Street story prioritizes white peoples' perspective. According to that story, a nineteen-year-old Black man, Dick Rowland, attempted to rape a white female elevator operator, seventeen-year-old Sarah Page, an incident that became the excuse for 1.8 million dollars in property loss (27 million in today's dollars) and race riots. White newspapers told this version, and so it became the official record. But there are several counterstories, including one that said Rowland and Page were in a romantic relationship, and that Page was pregnant; this was later proven false. A more likely story is that Rowland tripped when entering the elevator, stepped on Page's toe, and brushed against her, making her scream. This seems the most likely version.[1] Page never filed charges and denied that her clothes were torn or that she was scratched, as the papers had reported.

Whatever the facts, this Drexel elevator encounter between two teenagers never warranted the resulting death and destruction. Such a disproportionate response can only be understood in its historical context. This was an era of lynching and the KKK in Tulsa. The financial and social success of Greenwood fostered racism, economic jealousy, and land lust. This was a united community whose agency was demonstrated by the African American residents who marched to the jail where Rowland was held after he was arrested. They organized to prevent his lynching. These demands by African Americans infuriated local law enforcement, precipitating an argument at the courthouse. A swelling number of white men gathered, and a gun was discharged. A white mob of thousands carrying weapons formed. They chased the Black men back to Greenwood. Deplorable acts of domestic terrorism then ensued. For decades, the full story of Black Wall Street was silenced. Mass graves where the victims were buried also buried the story. Only survivors and ancestors kept them alive.

POSITIONALITY—WHO TELLS THE STORY?

On Election Day in 2016, white evangelical voters supported Donald Trump and the Republican Party by an 81 percent margin; this was the block of voters that pushed Trump over the edge to victory. The winning candidate played on the perception that America's changing demographics and cultural values were a threat to the country's way of life. The story told was that America was in decline, and Trump was the last hope. The evangelical community responded with fear and rage.[2] This same fear and rage is being fanned by erroneous perceptions of CRT.

Perception is a complicated psychological process that is unique to each individual. Each of us has different cognitive schemata, mental constructs by which we organize meaning. Because of our unique life experiences, we structure those meanings differently; we therefore look at the world through distinct lenses.[3] Some Americans saw Trump as the last hope to rescue the country from immorality, restore traditional values, and protect it against immigrants. Others perceived Trump as racist, sexist, and a threat to democracy. Narrative habits establish our patterns of perception and frame the way we see reality. These habits are reinforced through silos of media outlets, both television and social media, that claimed a position and bias that repeatedly played to the chosen perspective.

Trump was good at telling a story about white America's decline and the loss of America's way of life. Coded is the centrality of whiteness, because for Native Americans and African Americans, that way of life was genocide, slavery, Jim Crow, unequal opportunity, and institutional racism. From this perspective, America was never great. Trump told the "Make America Great Again" story from the white man's perspective, and prioritized white peoples' fears and concerns. Tragically, white Christian conservatives were the audience that predominantly embraced Trump's storytelling, with regular white church-attending Americans voting for him *en masse* in the 2020 Presidential race.[4] The divergence in political perceptions occurs along racial and religious lines.

White Christian conservatives perceive America differently, and this difference funds the controversy over CRT. CRT is resisted because it challenges a white positionality—American history told from a white perspective, the preaching and reading of the Bible from white theologians' eyes, and the canon of English literature by white writers. Challenging white centrism is where the pushback comes from. Wendell Berry, the prolific author and environmentalist, reflects on this phenomenon:

> It occurs to me that, for a man whose life from the beginning has been conditioned by the lives of black people, I have had surprisingly little to say about them in my writings. . . . [I]t has been an avoidance. . . . [I]t is the silence with which white men in this country have surrounded the anguish implicit in their racism.[5]

There is the silence again. Berry attributes it to white peoples' anguish about their own racism. CRT speaks to the silence in its tenet of counter-storytelling elevating the voices of people of color—shifting and undermining the white hegemonic status quo. It is a response to erasure of minority narratives. This includes the stories of Native, Black, Mexican, and Asian Americans, as well as recent immigrants. Mari Matsuda calls them stories from the "bottom up."[6]

Stories, parables, and narratives are powerful ways of upsetting mindsets—the myths, presuppositions, received wisdoms, and collective norms in which legal and political discourse reside. The underdog is heard. Counterstories prompt us to walk in other peoples' shoes, broaden our cognitive schemata, and ask questions about our own assumptions.[7] So instead of seeing the immigrant at the border as a threat to jobs or the American way of life, we see the contributions immigrants make to family values, community, our food, and our faith. CRT and legal storytelling create cognitive dissonance, challenging how we understand the law and race. But counter-storytelling began long before CRT. Jesus told counterstories.

JESUS AND COUNTER-STORYING

The dominant white American narrative of Jesus is that he was apolitical. This is the unexamined story. It is the institutional story. It has been repeated enough to become the church's reality. However, this narrative does not ring true with history or Jesus's own words. As a Jew, Jesus was oppressed by the Romans. He was marginalized and favored the poor. Such was Jesus's positionality. Rome and the Herodian dynasty dominated the Jewish people. Both entities were threatened by Jesus's popularity with the poor and talk of the kingdom of God. They feared social upheaval.

These fears were not unwarranted. Luke 4: 16–30 depicts Jesus standing in the temple in his hometown, Nazareth, and reading the scriptures. He chooses Isaiah 61:1–2, which identifies him as prophet bringing a core message of social reversal: "The Spirit of the Lord is upon me [Jesus], to preach good news to the poor, to set prisons free, and give sight to the blind, and set the oppressed free." In other words, those dominated and enslaved physically, economically, and spiritually can anticipate liberation. This revolutionary talk is the thrust of Jesus's stated mission.[8]

At first, the small hometown synagogue audience seems impressed, but as he goes on, they become increasing irate. It becomes apparent that his talk is subversive, moving from the spiritual to the social. He tells two more counterstories, one about a widow, the other about a leper in the times of Elijah and Elisha. In the first story, Elijah, instead of comforting Israel's widows, went to a woman in Sidon, a foreign country, to help. In the second story, Elisha, instead of curing Israel's many lepers, cures an enemy and brutal army commander and foreigner, Naaman, the Syrian. These are counterstories because they are in opposition to the standard Bible reading, taking the position of the oppressed and giving voice to their experiences. Jesus's perspective is compassion for the outsider, our enemies, and the stranger. In today's context, it translates to the immigrant, the prisoner, the homeless—the others. This counterstory reverses the idea that worshipping in the temple or being part of a certain church means God's favor; the last will be first. God has a special interest in the outsider.

Listening to Jesus, the unsettling meaning became clear to his audience: We need to alter our economics, our interests, and our neighborhoods to accommodate those different from us in support of justice and equity. Our lifestyles are challenged. Counterstories frequently evoke resistance and anger. Jesus so angered the crowd that they became a mob and drove Jesus out of town, attempting to kill him by lynching and throwing him over a cliff. This leads the reader to believe, as many biblical scholars have maintained, that Jesus called for social revolution, not only personal transformation. In many South and Central American countries, this is the dominant understanding.[9] Counterstories can be dangerous business, as evidenced by many martyred South American priests and nuns in their alliance with the poor.

One last observation: It is of consequence that Jesus spoke the words of revolution in the temple, a space of spiritual worship. Commitment to Christ is both internal, of the heart, and external, a commitment to social justice. The two are inextricably linked in Jesus's core message.

The gentle, inoffensive Jesus that saves us from our sins and legalistic religious traditions, but stands clear of civil rights, collective organizing, challenging oppressive systems, and governmental protest, just does not comport with what the Gospel tells us about Jesus. Reading the Bible through the perception of the poor and oppressed uncovers revolutionary themes—exodus, promise, resurrection. Going toe-to-toe with Jewish political leaders and the Roman government branded Jesus an oppositionist and enemy of the state. In plain terms, "the land is not to be exploited any more, slaves are to be freed, debts are to be canceled, capital unjustly gained is to be redistributed. Any political, economic, social, or religious structures that perpetuate exploitation must change to create a society committed to the reversal of the plight of the poor and oppressed."[10] Herod and Pilate understood the threats that Jesus and his stories posed, so they eventually finished Jesus off—the botched killing that the temple crowd failed to do. Ultimately, Jesus was crucified by the Roman state as a political agitator.

Parables were Jesus's primary subversive speech—telling the way oppression serves the interests of the ruling class against the larger world of agrarian poor.[11] Parables are social analyses and theological reflection, the conscientization of the oppressed—a critical understanding of one's social reality through reflection and action.[12] Examples include the parable of the dishonest steward, which grapples with the cancelation of debt; the parable of the laborers in the vineyard, about blaming the victim and internalizing the oppressors' world; and the parable of the friend at midnight, about the agency of the poor to challenge dehumanization within its community. The parable of the unjust judge confronts social and gender boundaries with persistence and shamelessness.[13] The classic counterstory is the parable of the Good Samaritan, which tackles the oppression of the Samaritans and the question of whose responsibility it is to respond to a victim of a crime, a counterstory of race, ethnicity, class, and prejudice.

Freire and Gutierrez propose that the parables of Jesus presented characters, settings, and messages familiar to the agrarian poor and encoded the systems of oppression that controlled their lives, explaining to them the institutionalized discrimination that held them in bondage.[14] His audience would have understood the parables as both personal and political.

CRT AND COUNTER-STORYTELLING

Like the parables of Jesus, Derrick Bell used chronicles in his academic writing in the early years of CRT's development. He wrote fictionalized counterstories in *Harvard Law Review* to illustrate his core legal ideas. He also wrote *And We Are Not Saved* to expose how the law masks racial discrimination. Using fiction, Bell translated legal stories into human ones. He writes,

> Allegory offers a method of discourse that allows us to critique legal norms in an ironically contextualized way. Through the allegory, we can discuss legal doctrine in a way that does not replicate the abstractions of legal discourse. It provides therefore a more rich, engaging, and suggestive way of reaching the truth.[15]

That Bell's allegories resemble the parables of Jesus is not surprising. Bell came from the church and employed gospel music and scripture as well as parabolic writing in his legal scholarship. Among Bell's chronicles is "The Chronicle of the Sacrificed Black School Children."[16] This allegory, about the disappearance of all school-aged Black children in America, highlights how disastrous Brown vs. Board of Education was to many Black children, schools, and teachers. A legal policy made with the intention of eliminating segregation and equalizing educational opportunity instead undermined the education of the students it was designed to benefit. This is the kind of duplicity counter-storytelling is so good at exposing.

Bell's legal storytelling fostered criticism that his scholarship "lacked [the] objectivity and neutrality that characterizes academic scholarship in general and the law in particular."[17] But Bell generally ignored this criticism while writing nineteen science fiction stories. Today multiple genres of counter-storytelling are used in qualitative research methodology across academic disciplines. Early on, CRT and Bell embraced legal storytelling as an effective way of making injustice and oppression clear, very much as Jesus did.

RACE AND STORYTELLING

In America we tell stories about race. The dominant American narrative about race in and outside the church sounds like this:

Early in our history there was slavery, which was a terrible thing. Black people were brought to this country from Africa in chains and made to work in the fields. Some were viciously mistreated, which was, of course, an unforgivable wrong; others were treated kindly. Slavery ended with the Civil War, although many black people remained poor, uneducated, and outside the cultural mainstream. As the country's racial sensitivity to black peoples' plight increased, the vestiges of slavery were gradually eliminated by federal statutes and case law. Today, black people have many civil rights and are protected from discrimination in such areas as housing, public education, employment, and voting. The gap between black people and white people is steadily closing, although it may take some time for it to close completely. At the same time, it is important not to go too far in providing special benefits for black people. Doing so induces dependency and welfare mentality. It can also cause a backlash among innocent white victims of reverse discrimination. Most Americans are fair-minded individuals who harbor little racial prejudice. The few who do can be punished when they act on those beliefs.[18]

The church racial story includes all of the above with this appendix:

If you talk too much about race you cause dissension and are part of the problem and make racism worse. Things are getting better, and many churches are now interracial. Most people in the church and America are not racist; racism is a matter of a few bad apples and we must pray. The killings of black men by police are isolated incidents rather than part of a pattern. We need to move on from the past and stop talking about slavery; besides, the church was part of the abolition of slavery, and yes, there were some slave-holding Christians, but some slaves were saved through their masters, and some Christian slaves were treated like family. The solution is the salvation of souls; it is a matter of the heart. The church has created charities and urban missions. How can it be considered racist? If everyone was truly a Christian, a real Christian, then racism would go away. God will make change. Woke ideology and CRT are creeping into our churches, and it is insidious and dangerous. We need to preach the Gospel and save souls, not be woke and make social justice the Gospel.

Consciously or unconsciously, these dominant narratives permeate white people's thinking and that of some Black people, too. Contrary to the dominant white narrative, more talk about race is needed. Sometimes it is scary for white people to hear the counter-stories because the stories can be angry and strongly worded. Yet accepting and realizing that we are all wounded by our racial history is a good approach to intentional listening. "Counter-storytelling and CRT are ways of pulling off the scab so the wound can be cleaned and heal."[19] Churches ought to be safe spaces to talk about pain. The ritual of testifying is opening up—honesty, forgiveness, repentance, understanding, support, and reparations. It's the way of the church. The counterstory is in a sense a testimony to what people have experienced regarding race and acknowledging that as a nation we are all scarred. And in so doing, it also recognizes that people of color's collective lived experiences are often distressing, institutionalized and prevalent, yet unique to the individual.

RACIAL AND THEOLOGICAL GASLIGHTING

Listening, though, is hard work. American writer James Baldwin, who grew up in the Black church, knew what it was like to go unheard:

> What is most terrible is that American white men are not pre-pared to believe my version of the story, to believe it happened. In order to avoid believing that, they have set up in them-selves a fantastic system of evasion, denials, and justifications, which system is about to destroy their grasp of reality, which is another way of saying their moral sense.[20]

And that is just about right. The white church needs to do the hard work of listening and believing the experience of Black people in America—their theologians and churches. And as Baldwin says, the alternative is that the church will lose its moral compass. Arguably, the American church has lost its moral way—the soul of a nation—already.[21] Challenges to the dominant story are necessary.

Slaveholding was wrong and no amount of paternalistic rational-izing about slaves being part of the slaveholders' family alters that fact. In the words of Frederick Douglass, writing about the religious conversion of his slave master:

> Being the slave of a religious master is the greatest calamity that could befall me. For of all slaveholders with whom I have ever met, religious slaveholders are the worst. I have ever found them the meanest and basest, the cruelest and cowardly, of all others.[22]

Douglass erroneously thought that once his master was saved, he would have shown compassion. Instead, his master became crueler. In Lenny Duncan's *Dear Church: A Love Letter from a Black Preacher to the Whitest Denomination in the U.S.*, the author speaks their counterstory: "I know grace is why so many Black Lutherans put up with thousands of macroaggressions that feel like death by a thousand tiny cuts in this church. . . . [T]he almost universal experience of Black leaders in the Evangelical Lutheran church of America is one of suffering the subtle and not-so-subtle effects of systemic racism."[23] Douglass's and Duncan's perspectives, although separated by almost 150 years, sound eerily similar.

It doesn't seem like racism is past in the church, or like not talking about it will make it go away. Instead, it seems like a lot of racial gaslighting is going on. Racial gaslighting is the act of undermining and belittling the feelings of marginalized individuals. It is a form of abuse and psychological manipulation.[24] It portrays an environment as inclusive and welcoming when the words and experiences of people of color contradict this portrayal. Racial gaslighting makes the victim question and doubt their feelings and positions on race because they are invalidated.

Gaslighting does not only happen between two individuals; it also happens within organizations, systems, and churches. In some ways the recent denial of CRT and the claims that CRT is incongruent with the Gospel are spiritual abuse and theological gaslighting. It is psychological manipulation to use the Bible as a weapon to deny systemic racism and the lived experiences of Black people in the church.[25]

GASLIGHTING BLACK THEOLOGY

Esau McCaulley is an Anglican priest and New Testament scholar at Weaton College, and was racially gaslighted during his evangelical seminary training.

> The more time I spent among evangelicals, the more I realized that those spaces can subtly and not so subtly breed a certain disdain for what they see as the "uncouthness" of black culture. We were told that our churches weren't sound theologically because our clergy did not always speak the language of the academy. In my evangelical seminary almost all the authors we read were white men. . . . I was told that the social gospel had corrupted Black Christianity. . . . [There was] a general agreement on a certain reading of American history that downplayed injustice and a gentlemen's agreement to remain largely silent on current issues of racism and systemic injustice.[26]

McCaulley's experience is not unique. McCaulley was able to evolve during his graduate education to an understanding that Black theology is a counter-interpretation to whites' theological perspectives on race and the Bible. Black theology is in large measure a response to racism. Historically the Black encounter with the Bible was different, a counter-reading that prompted Black people to form their own churches and denominations.[27]

The dominant white story is that Africans first heard of Christianity through slavery, and that Christianity has European roots. This is untrue. The three major centers of early Christianity were Alexandria, Antioch, and Rome. Augustine and Tertullian, two of antiquity's greatest Christian thinkers, came from North Africa.[28] Black theology corrects Eurocentric historical biases placed on the scriptures.[29] It is a framework for acknowledging the suffering of Black people in America, as well as people in the Global South, through a God and Bible that address this suffering. Black theology, by countering dominant white narratives, understands the Bible as being on the side of the poor and marginalized.[30] From Exodus to the Gospels, it is consistent in its themes of liberation and solidarity with the powerless, the outsiders, and the weak, with its focus on gentiles, lepers, the poor, women, harlots, the demonized, and publicans. Black theology reminds us that individuals and communities bring their own lived experiences, perceptions, and historical context as they read the scriptures. Through Black theology, white people and white theologians are invited to be converted to the perspective of the marginalized.[31]

Regrettably, Black theology has been gaslit by the white religious establishment and even some portions of the Black community. That is, it has been ignored, dismissed as too radical, not scholarly, and anti-biblical (read: anti-Eurocentric). But Black theology is not dependent on white perceptions or value judgments.[32] According to James H. Cone, considered the father of Black liberation theology, "Black theology [aims] to analyze the black man's condition in the light of God's revelation in Jesus Christ with the purpose of creating a new understanding of black dignity among black people, and providing the necessary soul in that people, to destroy white racism."[33] Cone wanted to speak on behalf of the voiceless Black masses in the name of Jesus because the white church and its theology distorted the Gospel's message of comprehensive liberation.

BANNING BOOKS—THE NEGATION OF THE COUNTERSTORY

The anti-CRT paranoia is fueling a renewed state book banning. From 2020 to 2021 the number of banned books doubled.[34] Most are fiction and nonfiction, with protagonists of color and plots and themes that include race, ethnicity, gender identity, and sexual orientation. Additional books are centered on American history from the positionality of African American, Asian, Hispanic, and immigrant authors.

Why are books banned? Most often the books are determined by someone in power to be subversive and harmful. This is not new.

Stories have long been used in the struggle for racial reform, from the early slave songs, underground railroad lyrics, narratives, and verse.[35] According to the ACLU, the banning of books by Blacks is ongoing with a recent uptick:

> The racist campaign of repression against Black authors has never really stopped—only ebbed from time to time. Today, however, this campaign has roared back into life with a relentless effort to remove Black-authored books from libraries, race-conscious subjects from curricula, and any mention of racism from our collective history. This is partly an obvious backlash to the racial justice movement sparked by the murders of George Floyd, Breonna Taylor, Ahmaud Arbery, and countless others—but it's also just the latest chapter in a long story of racist censorship.[36]

Stories threaten existing arrangements and the beneficiaries of the current economic, religious, and political establishment. Stories are tools of survival, liberation, healing, and self-preservation—"stories humanize us."[37] This is why they are seen as so dangerous. Anti-CRT laws and book banning go hand in hand, endorsed by top-down state legislation supported by national conservatives, with silence from churches in many cases.

Book banning is a defensive act because subordinated groups telling counter-stories is powerful. Reading the Bible, although not a banned book in America, is the reading of a counterstory—the story of a first-century lynching of a political agitator committed to the poor, oppressed, and marginalized. It is the story of individual and collective freedom. It is the story that threatened the religious leaders and political empire of Christ's time and ultimately cost Jesus his life. Translated to America in the twenty-first century, it is a counterstory to the dominant church narrative of the Gospel as a solely spiritual transformation and a confrontation to white theology and supremacy in the church.

NOTES

1 Johnson, *Black Wall Street.*
2 Jones, *White Christian America.*
3 Piaget and Inhelder, *The Psychology of the Child.*
4 Nortey, "Most White Americans ."
5 Berry, *The Hidden Wound.*
6 Matsuda, "Looking to the Bottom."
7 Delgado and Stefancic, *Critical Race Theory.*
8 Brown, *Unexpected News.*
9 Brown.
10 Brown.
11 Herzog, *Parables as Subversive Speech.*
12 Herzog.
13 Herzog.
14 Herzog.
15 Bell, *And We Are Not Saved.*
16 Bell.
17 Albert-Howe, "Counterstorytelling."
18 Delgado, "Storytelling for Oppositionists."
19 J. R. Chaney, personal communication, September 19, 2022.
20 Glaude, *Begin Again.*
21 Biden, "Remarks."
22 Douglass, *Narrative.*
23 Duncan, *Dear Church.*
24 Rodrigues, Mendenhall, and Clancy, "There's Realizing."
25 Edmiston, "Theological Gaslighting."
26 McCaulley, *Reading While Black.*
27 McCaulley.
28 McCaulley; Isichei, *A History of Christianity in Africa.*
29 Brown, *Blackening of the Bible.*
30 Brown.
31 Brown.
32 Cone, *A Black Theology of Liberation.*
33 Cone, *Black Theology & Black Power.*
34 "Banned in the USA."
35 Delgado, "Storytelling for Oppositionists."
36 ACLU, "Banned Books by Black Authors."
37 Delgado, "Storytelling for Oppositionists."

CHAPTER NINE

Black Lives Matter

"Sometimes I just want to scream, church!"

—Chisholm, 2021

Father Gregory Chisholm's wail reverberated through St. Patrick's Cathedral at the opening of his Black History Month homily: "God knows I have felt like screaming every day of the last year." The combination of Covid-19, the murder of George Floyd, the angry white men and women of the January 6th Capitol assault, and the historical skepticism of Black people about government-provided vaccines drove Chisholm to shout, "I am an angry Black man."[1] The racial disparities in healthcare, Black peoples' historically driven skepticism of the medical profession, and the policing of Black men remind us again of America's disregard for Black bodies. Chisholm did not mention CRT or the Black Lives Matter movement, but the spirit and thrust of his powerful homily embraces both.

Chisholm, a highly regarded Catholic priest, calls out Americans as the most sin-sick people on God's earth because of racism, while identifying Black Christians as the keepers of the faith. Christian African Americans are true believers, and continue to this day to show an uncommon commitment to God despite questioning His periodic silence. They have become the face of God in this country.[2]

ABRAHAM—THE FIRST ANGRY BLACK MAN*

Listening to this homily, I turned to my husband, another six-foot-tall Black man, and saw him brush tears from his eyes. I thought of how many Black men and women have shed these tears. The prophet Abraham could have been the first. God asked of Abraham the unthinkable, to kill his only son Isaac in obedience and in sacrifice to God. Ultimately, God stayed Abraham's hand and Isaac was spared, but Abraham must have felt anger and rage for the choice God asked of him. Anger, rage, and protest are natural responses to injustice.

Black Lives Matter exists in this tradition. It is a response to patterns of injustice and historical Black pain over disregard for Black peoples' bodies. The Black Lives Matter movement (not to be confused with the BLM organization) was born with the BLM hashtag following the acquittal of George Zimmerman, who killed seventeen-year-old Trayvon Martin in Sandford, Florida in 2012. Trayvon was unarmed and was murdered while walking to his father's home after buying snacks at a convenience store. Following the acquittal of Zimmerman, who was on neighborhood watch the evening of Trayvon's death, three young Black women, artist-activists Alicia Garza, Patrisse Khan-Cullors, and Opal Tometi, created the BLM movement on social media in protest to the disregard for Black lives. Then in the summer of 2014, the movement responded to the killing of Michael Brown by police in Ferguson, Missouri. Local BLM groups began to spring up across the country and throughout the world. These grassroots organizations support families of people killed by police, organize protests, and hold police accountable.[3]

Like Abraham, BLM is a movement created in response to anger and rage. BLM is driven by fury at the unresponsiveness of law enforcement and government officials, the militarization of the police, and a society that undervalues Black people. From a CRT lens it protests the effects of the war on drugs in poor neighborhoods,

---

* Abraham was from Ur the land of Chaldeans in Mesopotamia, modern-day Iraq. He was likely a person of color.

the traumatization and jailing of Black and brown children for minor offenses, the cheap labor extracted from prisoners, expansion of prison facilities (both public and for-profit) to provide poor white people with jobs in rural communities, the placement of the mentally ill in prison, the acquittal of police officers even in the presence of video evidence, and that the US has 5 percent world's population but 20 percent of the prison population.[4] According to the ACLU, "Since 1970, our incarcerated population has increased by 500 percent—two million people are in jail or prison today, far outpacing population growth and crime. This population is disproportionately Black and Hispanic. One out of every three Black boys born today can expect to go to prison in his lifetime, as can one of every six Latino boys—compared to one of every seventeen white boys."

Despite reasons for anger and rage, BLM is by and large a peaceful movement, although framed by a few Christian authors as "promoting social destruction and physical violence."[5] Like CRT, BLM faces both misunderstanding and opposition in the church.

MISNOMERS AND CHURCH OPPOSITION

Perhaps the most egregious misnomer is that the BLM movement and protests are violent and dangerous. This is wrong. According to several reports by the nonprofit organization, The Armed Conflict Location and Event Data Project, which tracks violent protest around the world, 94 percent of BLM protests are peaceful.[6] In the report's words, "The BLM movement has remained overwhelmingly non-violent."[7] In contrast, right-wing militant social protest in the US are twice as often (14 percent of the time) violent. The data also reports that despite the nonviolent nature of most BLM protests, police take a heavy hand against these protesters as compared to other demonstrators. This is not to say that there have been no violent incidents associated with BLM protests. Protests against the police killing of Breonna Taylor in Louisville, Kentucky are a case in point, but Louisville is not the norm. Additionally, incidents of violence or destruction occurred primarily when right-wing groups engaged with pro-BLM demonstrators.[8]

The FBI was also misled about the nature of the movement and created a "Black Identity Extremist Movement" program that surveilled BLM activists solely on the basis of race. In 2018–2019, the operation was called "Iron Fist"; the FBI spent money and time investigating BLM, only to find no terrorist threat. Active white supremacist groups were not picked up by the FBI; think January 6th. Ironically in the wake of the 2020 election, many BLM advocates received death threats from these supremacist groups. Six men connected with the Ferguson protests were found mysteriously dead in later years.[9]

White supremacists account for far greater numbers of domestic terrorist attacks than any other group and are responsible for a growing proportion of extremist violence worldwide.[10] During the height of BLM protests, the FBI looked for terrorism in the wrong places and among the wrong people.[11] Tragically, domestic terrorists can be more likely found among the churched than unchurched:

> If you were recruiting for a white supremacist cause on a Sunday morning, you'd likely have more success hanging out in the parking lot of an average white Christian church—evangelical Protestant, mainline Protestant, or Catholic—than approaching white people sitting out services at the local coffee shop.[12]

This supports findings by the Public Religion Research Institute that attending church and identifying as a Christian increases the likelihood of holding racist attitudes.[13] These same conclusions were reached by the Emerson and Smith studies two decades earlier.[14]

A second point of opposition to BLM involves the traditionalist church's struggle over LGBTQ issues and the concern over BLM founders' sexual orientations and support for LGBTQ equity. Opponents see this as the dismantling of the biblical definition of family.[15] To be clear, Black Lives Matter refers to a network of loosely connected local and decentralized advocacy groups (both online and face-to-face) primarily focused on racial justice and police brutality. Their focus is not on dismantling family structures, although most groups support liberation for all marginalized groups including LGBTQ individuals.[16]

The BLM founders are not professed atheists or irreligious, and there is no indication that they have a disregard for religion or hold beliefs antithetical to Christianity. Alicia Garza, the founder attributed with creating the BLM slogan, is African American and Jewish. Patrisse Khan-Cullors grew up as a Jehovah's Witness and was raised by a single mother. Her family was shunned by the church because of her mother's pregnancy, but despite this, Khan-Cullors maintained faith. She writes that her exodus from church is not a flight from faith—nor is it for many young BLM supporters.[17] Besides being one of the founders of the movement, Khan-Cullors is an ordained minister with a religious studies degree at UCLA and practices philosophy, having studied with a concentration in Abrahamic traditions. She practices Ifa, a Yoruban spiritual tradition of West Africa. Co-founder Ayo Tometi was born in Phoenix, Arizona, to Nigerian immigrant parents and was influenced by liberation theology. She regards faith as an integral part of her life. Her family is Christian, and her parents started a church for African immigrants.[18] BLM has been identified as a "religion of protest" for many millennials who have been disillusioned with traditional churches and for some it is a fight for Black lives driven by spiritual ideals.[19]

Olga Segura, in *Black Lives Matter and the Catholic Church,* addresses criticisms, making the case that BLM is neither an extremist agenda nor a contradiction of faith. Instead, it is an acting out of faith and the social teaching of Jesus, who continuously worked for the dignity of the "least of these." BLM are feet on the ground of faith.[20]

Finally, the Black Lives Matter Global Network Foundation, the steward organization of the movement and loosely affiliated with hundreds of local groups, has been under scrutiny for lack of financial transparency. But as of February 2021, the Foundation opened up its finances for full transparency, as well as to address grievances by the movement's grassroots organizers. They questioned decision-making and accountability, especially after the murder of George Floyd, when donations to the foundation increased substantially.[21] This follows several years of tensions between local BLM chapters and the national foundation. In September 2022, twenty-five local BLM groups filed a complaint against the foundation for citing mismanagement and shutting local organization out of decision-making.[22] These growing pains connect back to the inner tensions of different philosophical and organizational factions during the civil rights movement, which were exacerbated by government operatives. This kind of discrediting appears to be similarly aimed at BLM.

ALL LIVES MATTER VS. BLACK LIVES MATTER

All Lives Matter is a retort to Black Lives Matter and is associated with conservative views rejecting the claims of BLM. The very urge to say "All Lives Matter" betrays a misunderstanding of race in America. It is a downplaying of the valid risks that Black people, in particular young Black men, face when encountering police. BLM does not suggest that all lives are not important; instead that there are unique problems in Black communities as a result of white supremacy. And it does not mean that Black lives matter *more*.

Protecting the lives of one group does not diminish the rights of other groups. The issue is equity. All Lives Matter is defensive rhetoric suggesting that we can dismiss accusations of white privilege or supremacy. It silences Black voices by taking away the emphasis and battles at hand—police brutality and unequal treatment of Black people in the criminal justice system.[23]

In clarifying this rhetorical fallacy, consider the Covid pandemic and the advertising "Get Your Covid Vaccination" and "Getting Vaccinated Matters." These slogans focused on vaccinations, but did not mean that you shouldn't wear a mask, maintain social distance, or wash your hands. Nor did these slogans mean that you shouldn't get a flu shot or polio vaccine. In other words, if something matters, it does not mean that nothing else matters. It is about focus, not exclusion. For too long Black people have been disproportionately impacted by police violence, hyper-criminalization, and over-policing, as well as systemic policies that disadvantage minority communities. That is the message of BLM. Once racism no longer exists and all lives truly matter equally, there will be no need for BLM.

Similarly, regarding "Blue Lives Matter," BLM never meant that police officers do not matter and that responsible policing is not necessary. Because BLM is a direct response to police behavior, it makes sense that some supporters might respond defensively to law enforcement. It is human and healthy to protest individuals, policies, and practices that have harmed you. This does not mean you think law enforcement is not needed. Is it possible to respect the police, have police officers in one's family, understand the need for law enforcement, and yet also see the need for reform? Yes. The slogan "Defund the Police" has been misinterpreted. It does not mean that we do not need police in times of emergency and to secure safe communities. Few in the BLM movement would argue that. However, it does mean that we should explore alternatives to policing: youth recreation programs, mental health counseling, substance abuse treatment, housing, gun control, et cetera.[24] This is common sense. It is more a matter of redistribution of funds to support initiatives that will aid the police in doing their jobs.

The BLM movement's main focus has been policing, even though in its global reach it also addresses the rights of women, the LGBTQ community, immigrants, refugees, indigenous people, and disabled people. Precipitated by the deaths of Trayvon Martin, Michael Brown, Eric Garner, Breonna Taylor, and George Floyd at the hands of law enforcement, BLM began. These murders are the result of a long and sad history of American policing embedded in slavery and racism. CRT is again an effective lens to understand the systemic policing of Black men and women.

The origins of modern-day policing are slave patrols in the early 1700s Carolinas. The goal of these patrols was to terrorize slaves, prevent them from uprising, and return runaway slaves to their owners.

These patrols continued until the Civil War. During Reconstruction, they were replaced by militia groups, who terrorized freed slaves and enforced the Black Codes. These were state and local laws restricting the rights of Black people: voting, traveling after dark, talking too loudly, walking on the wrong side of the street, speaking to white women, et cetera. If one of these rules were broken, public lynching could result at the whim of citizen and police control. Lynching and the Black Codes continued into the 1950s.

Through a CRT perspective, it is not hard to connect the case of Ahmaud Arbery, a twenty-five-year-old Black man who was murdered in his neighborhood while jogging, to this nefarious past. Arbery's murder in 2020 was the result of domestic terrorism and vigilante "justice"—citizens taking the law into their own hands. It was a modern-day lynching. Research indicates that Black and brown adolescents and children experience over-policing everywhere from their school to their neighborhood. Pervasive among Black youth is everyday surveillance and resulting trauma. There is a long history of not seeing Black children as children. Unnecessary policing of Black youth includes excessive stop and frisks, forcible handling, racial stereotyping, and unnecessary search and seizure. Policing is not a neutral event; the mere presence of policing affects children and is stressful.[25] According to America's pediatrician, Dr. Benjamin Spock, "Most middle-class white people have no idea what it feels like to be subjected to police who are routinely suspicious, rude, belligerent, and brutal."[26]

From this legacy of police brutality, CRT highlights the systemic discrimination within the criminal justice system, from arrest to prosecution, conviction, and sentencing. To this day, Black and brown people have been excessively charged while police officers who break the law are under-prosecuted. Prosecutors work with police and often have ongoing working relationships with them; police officers are therefore infrequently held accountable. This is because as elected officials, prosecutors are afforded great discretion in deciding whether to charge, and what crime to charge, all while law enforcement officers enjoy the blanket protections of qualified immunity. Even when charges are filed, police officers are seldom convicted.[27] From a CRT lens, structural racism and injustice are embedded historically and systematically in all aspects of the criminal justice system.

Cell phones and video recordings now make it possible to document police mistreatment, bringing awareness to what has been happening for hundreds of years. Just as the murder of Emmett Till sparked the civil rights movement, the Black Lives Matter movement began after the murders of Black individuals at the hands of the police. This rekindled awareness of the need for police reform. Reform is no easy or fast process, but recent signs of reform breed hope.

Structural reform of policing is not unfamiliar to the New Testament, In fact, McCaulley understands the apostle Paul's words to point to a Christian theology of policing. Roman soldiers during Christ's time were the equivalent to police today, and Paul's concerns were not for the individual soldier's behavior, but the attitude of the empire and the influence the state had on individual soldiers. Paul's words speak to structural reform and the government's role in not being a source of fear for its citizens.[28]

BLACK LIVES MATTER, FRANKLIN GRAHAM, AND THE EVANGELICAL CHURCH

Franklin Graham III, the son of evangelist Billy Graham and president and CEO of the Billy Graham Evangelistic Association, could benefit from a lesson on CRT. On March 12, 2015, Graham wrote a Facebook post that attributed police killings of young Black men to the victims' bad parental upbringing and the men's need to learn to "OBEY" authority. He said that the solution was "simple." In his words,

> Listen up—Black people, whites, Latinos, and everybody else.... [M]ost police shootings can be avoided. It comes down

to respect for authority and obedience. If a police officer tells you to stop, you stop. If a police officer tells you to put your hands in the air, you put your hands in the air.... It's as simple as that.... [E]ven if you think the police officer is wrong—YOU OBEY.[29]

Sadly, 200,000 "likes" to the post were recorded, presumably from Christians. Graham's retort belies a simplistic perspective on race that faults the victim. It demonstrates no understanding that police brutality in America is related to power and race. And it shows no understanding of the systemic racism demonstrated by our criminal justice system.

As it so often does, the evangelical church in this case made racism about one isolated incident, extracting it from sociological and historical context and ignoring recurring patterns of discrimination and police terrorism. In protest, several Christian leaders responded to Franklin in an open letter by challenging his ignorance:

It is not that simple. As a leader in the church, you are called to be an ambassador of reconciliation. The fact that you identify a widely acknowledged social injustice as "simple" reveals your lack of empathy and understanding of the depth of sin that some in the body have suffered under the weight of our broken justice system.[30]

Following Graham's "simple" logic, and without frameworks like CRT to inform thinking, the conclusions become: Black people do not obey and Black people do not have a respect for authority; therefore, they deserve what happens. Beyond this statement related to BLM, Graham's website lambastes CRT. It appears that Franklin Graham is preoccupied with issues of race. Perceptions like Franklin's repeatedly go back to the individual while avoiding discussion and admission of systemic racism.[31] Perhaps this is why CRT seems hard to accept. If CRT is embraced, all our systems and structures will need examination through the eyes of race. Then our institutions may need to change. Changing our minds is hard work.

JESUS AND BLACK LIVES MATTER

In tandem with finishing this chapter, my husband and I are watching the final congressional hearing on the January 6th Capitol riots. Comparisons between the treatment of Black Lives Matter protesters and the Capitol rioters uncover the over-policing of BLM events, and the under-response by law enforcement in the case of January 6th, despite the police receiving prior warnings about heavily armed protesters that day.

The contrast is quite striking. January 6th rioters attacked and maimed police, desecrated and defecated in the halls of Congress, carried Confederate flags, and terrorized staff and elected representatives. They verbally threatened to hang Vice President Mike Pence and murder House Speaker Nancy Pelosi and others. Their goal was to stop the certification of the election and, with it, the peaceful transfer of power.

In comparison, while there has been destruction of private property during BLM protests, most are peaceful. The majority of BLM protesters are unarmed. BLM's goals for protests are not to undermine democracy or the will of the people, but instead to end police brutality against Black people and provide support and protection for the brutalized. And yet, which protest movement does the church decry as Marxist, godless, and even demonic? Black Lives Matter. And which protest is the church relatively silent about? January 6th, led by the Proud Boys and Oath Keepers, openly white supremacist groups.

Research by Robert A. Pape, director of the Chicago Project on Security and Threats, finds that contrary to popular myth, the economic downturn in the country was not the main driver for the January 6th protests. Surprisingly, many of the rioters were not lower- or middle-class white people as portrayed. It was not a class-based riot. Instead, the "great replacement theory" was the main impetus; rioters accused the Democratic Party of replacing the white population (the current electorate) with new voters from the Global South.[32] This research goes on to explain that racial resentment and partisanship play large roles in the embrace of replacement theory.

Troublingly consistent with Pape's findings is research that finds that white evangelical Protestants, white mainline Protestants, and white Catholics who attend church regularly hold racist attitudes more often than non-church goers, and white churches are institutional spaces that preserve and transmit white supremacist perceptions.[33] Tragically, the local churches hardly push back against the white supremacist groups that spearheaded January 6th, and yet it seems acceptable for some pastors to preach that the Black Lives Matter movement is subversive.

Patrisse Khan-Cullors states, "I have lived my life between the twin terrors of poverty and the police."[34] As a small child, she watched her thirteen- and fourteen-year-old brothers' encounters with violence-prone police officers. They were harassed for playing in the alley or laughing too loud. She speaks of the omnipresence of the police in her neighborhood—they were never friendly, never spoke to the children or guided them across the street, and made it clear they didn't like her very much.

She was arrested for the first time at twelve for smoking marijuana in her Black neighborhood in Los Angeles, but she felt police never arrested white children at her school in a white neighborhood for the same offense. She and other Black youth were called *super predators*, and as an adult she and her fellow protesters are now labeled *terrorists* and subversives. And yet, the slayers of Emmett Till; the Birmingham Church bombers who killed Addie Mae Collins, Denise McNair, Carole Robertson, and Cynthia Wesley; the shooter at the Charleston Church; and white school shooters are seldom if ever labeled as such.[35]

Ironically, the placard atop Jesus's cross during his execution labeled him as subversive.[36] BLM is about change, and so was Jesus.

Jesus tackled racial, ethnic, gender, economic, and religious issues head-on and was executed as a subversive accused of challenging law and order.

The BLM movement raises many crucial questions for the church, even beyond race and policing. Why have so many young people gravitated to BLM while at the same time leaving the church? How will the church negotiate gender identification, same-sex marriages, and leadership questions going forward? When will the issue of gender equality be understood in the church? One wonders if the decline in church membership, particularly among the youth, is not in part a result of the church's inability to evolve and grow around issues of social justice.[37] Some may not be losing faith, but are losing faith in the church, as is the case for many LGBTQ believers.[38]

Michael Brown's autopsy in Ferguson revealed that he was not only shot in the hand and chest, but also twice on the top of his head. His body lay in the hot Missouri sun for four-and-a-half hours following his murder—dishonored without dignity.[39] This tragic death mobilized the BLM movement. When looking through the lens of CRT, Ferguson can be easily seen as a Black community of 21,000 residents, one that was systematically extorted and abused by police through minor parking and traffic citations and policies of taxation that kept the community poor and over-policed. Until recently, the police chief presided over the Ferguson municipal court. Michael Brown became just one more tragic casualty of a racist system.

I can only imagine that Jesus would have defied authorities and walked onto the street during those four hours and picked up Michael Brown's body in his arms. And decidedly, Jesus would have protested, holding up a Black Lives Matter sign for all to see.

NOTES

1 Gregory Chisholm, "Black History Month Homily."
2 Gregory Chisholm.
3 Segura, *Birth of a Movement.*
4 Khan-Cullors, *When They Call You a Terrorist*; "Mass Incarceration."

5 Strachan and MacArthur, *Christianity and Wokeness.*
6 The Armed Conflict Location and Event Data Project, "2020 Annual Report," "2021 Annual Report."
7 The Armed Conflict Location and Event Data Project, "2021 Annual Report."
8 The Armed Conflict Location and Event Data Project, "2020 Annual Report."
9 Jim Salter, "A Puzzling Number."
10 Jones, *White Too Long.*
11 Blanchard and Graham, *Dear White Women.*
12 Jones, *White Too Long.*
13 Jones.
14 Emerson and Smith, *Divided by Faith.*
15 Addison, "Anti-Christian"; Strachan and MacArthur, *Christianity and Wokeness.*
16 Segura, *Birth of a Movement.*
17 Fort, "The Religion of Protest"; Khan-Cullors, *When They Call You a Terrorist.*
18 Segura, *Birth of a Movement.*
19 Jones, *The End of White Christian America.*
20 Segura, *Birth of a Movement.*
21 Levin, "Chapters Sue Global Foundation"; Morrison, "AP Exclusive."
22 Fox, "10 Fallacies."
23 Blanchard and Graham, *Dear White Women.*
24 Cobb and Guariglia, *The Essential Kerner Commission Report.*
25 Davis, *Policing the Black Man.*
26 Spock, *Decent and Indecent.*
27 Davis, *Policing the Black Man.*
28 McCaulley, *Reading While Black.*
29 Harper, "An Open Letter to Franklin Graham."
30 Harper.
31 Weeks, "Critical Race Theory."
32 Pape, "UChicago CPOST."
33 Jones, *White Too Long*; Emerson and Smith, *Divided by Faith.*
34 Khan-Cullors, *When They Call You a Terrorist.*
35 Khan-Cullors.
36 Brown, *Critical Race Theory.*
37 Gushee, *Still Christian*; Jones, *White Too Long.*
38 Jones; Gushee.
39 Khan-Cullors, *When They Call You a Terrorist.*

CHAPTER TEN

Intersectionality and CRT

"How came Jesus into the world? Through God who created him and woman who bore him. Man, where is your part?"

—Sojourner Truth

Perhaps one of the first to operationalize intersectionality was Sojourner Truth, a former slave and one of the country's most ardent abolitionists and Black feminists. Born into slavery in 1797, she ran away from her New York slave master in 1827 when he refused to set her free as he had promised. Truth experienced a dramatic religious conversion to Christianity and became an itinerant preacher, involving herself in the antislavery movement. In the 1850s she was also active in the women's rights movement until her death in 1883.

She is famous for her speech delivered at the 1851 Women's Rights Convention in Akron, Ohio when she challenged the audience. In her strong oratorical style, she claimed as much entitlement to the vote and equal rights as any white woman or Black man. At the time, only white men could vote. Truth befriended Susan B. Anthony and Elizabeth Cady Stanton, joining them in the woman's suffrage movement but later distancing herself. Stanton was not prepared to support the Black vote for men if women were denied their voting rights. Truth distanced herself because the language of the women's suffrage movement had become increasingly racist.[1] Not until 1920 would women get the right to vote, and even then discriminatory laws—especially in the South—would make it hard for Black women to exercise this right. Black men, meanwhile, were granted the right to vote in 1870.[2]

The Black abolitionist and former slave Frederick Douglass met Truth in Massachusetts around 1840 at the Northampton Association, an abolitionist community. Douglass liked Truth's oratory abilities but was patronizing and thought her to be uneducated and uncultured. In Truth's lived experience, "among Black people are women; among the women, there are Black people."[3] Truth embodies the concept of intersectionality, a tenet within CRT and at the same time a separate theory. Sojourner Truth experienced at least three levels of inequality in America and the church: race, gender, and class. Today intersectionality examines how multiple forms of identity and inequality are interconnected.

INTERSECTIONALITY DEFINED

The term *intersectionality* originated in the writings of Dr. Kimberlé Crenshaw, a legal scholar and a critical race theorist. In a 1989 article, she explained how the discrimination that African American women experience is not encompassed under US antidiscrimination legislation.[4] To win a lawsuit within this system, women had to make the case of discrimination on either race or gender, but could not make the case for both. There were blind spots in US antidiscrimination legislation that did not address the African American woman's experience of discrimination. Crenshaw's work addressed how Western feminism was often rooted in the experience of the white, heterosexual, middle-class woman. Crenshaw argued that there are multiple forms of discrimination that can be interrelated. Simply articulated:

Intersectionality is a concept that enables us to recognize the fact that perceived group membership can make people vulnerable to various forms of bias, yet because we are simultaneously members of many groups our complex identities can shape the specific way we each experience that bias.[5]

This definition is straightforward and commonsensical. Each of us has multiple identities that interact with others, with institutions, and with systems of oppression. Intersectionality within CRT highlights both how race and gender dynamics within institutions and institutional policy impact women and people of color.

STRACHAN'S ARGUMENT TO INTERSECTIONALITY

This concept appears troublesome for some conservative white male authors and church leaders, not only in Sojourner Truth's day but also in the twenty-first century. Owen Strachan is a case in point. As the author of twenty Christian books, provost and research professor at Grace Bible Theological Seminary, and senior fellow with the Family Research Council, he has a strong voice in the conservative Christian community. Strachan makes many arguments against intersectionality, but at their core is:

Although it rejects *binary* thinking in terms of the sexes, it is ironically binary to its core. You are either an oppressor in different areas of life, or you are oppressed. There is no middle ground. Your skin color and access to privilege determine which category you're in, not your character.[6]

Strachan is wrong. Intersectionality is all about complexity and offers plenty of middle ground. Individuals vary greatly in their experiences of access, privilege, and subjection to oppressive force; there is no one oppressor or one victim. Our interwoven identities create a complicated system of advantages, disadvantages, opportunities, with discrimination that varies according to one's life experiences. Second, intersectionality does not negate, address, or diminish character. Character matters—the moral and mental qualities and choices distinctive to each individual, their sense of right and wrong, and pursuant actions all matter. CRT and intersectionality do not subtract from this. Strachan is correct, however, in asserting that skin color and access to privilege are affected by the social constructs and groups to which one belongs.

In particular, the power dynamics and oppression of Black women are the crux of intersectionality and may account for the strong opposition to BLM in the American church. Intersectionality calls into question the strongholds of sexism and racism within society, including the church, and is a tool to analyze major interlocking systems of oppression. Granted, strong language is sometimes used when arguing for an understanding of intersectionality: toxic masculinity, oppressors, racist, white privilege, bigots, et cetera. Words matter, and intersectionality attempts to develop nuanced language used for critical analysis.

WOMANIST BIBLICAL INTERPRETATION

Despite the oppression of Black women, the scale of their faith and social justice advocacy can't be overstated. Black women are among the most religious demographic in this country. As mothers of the church and social activists driven by their faith, they exemplify the power of religious conviction:

> The faith of Black women gave them courage to fight, patience when they could not, and the hope that whatever they did, God would keep them from sinking down. God was the one reality that whites could not control and whose presence was found in unexpected places, doing surprising things.[7]

The term *womanist* comes from the writing of Alice Walker, who intersected feminism and racism to center advocacy for the rights of Black women. It originally comes from a Black colloquialism meaning *grown-up*, such as in the case of a mother telling her audacious daughter, "You acting womanish."[8] A womanist is a feminist woman of color impacted by the intersection of racism and sexism. As with the first suffragist movement, elements of 1960's Black Power, civil rights, and white feminist movements were not inclusive of Black women. Therefore, the womanist movement was born. This movement extended to the church, especially in the area of theology:

> As it relates to biblical studies, womanism has come to refer to a form of interpretation that joins together what many feel has been taken apart. Womanist scholars critique white feminism for its failure to examine its own privilege and for its neglect of issues of race. It also critiques Black theology because it focused on racism to the exclusion of sexism and patriarchy.[9]

Within biblical studies, the womanist scholar confronts and analyzes the domination and exploitation within the Bible (authored by men within a patriarchal society) and the biblical scholarship from the male and patriarchal perspective outside the Bible. This critical engagement with scripture from a womanist perspective is small but increasing as more women join the ordained ministry and the academy provides counter-storytelling and strategies for reading the Bible that assume an advocacy stance for women's liberation.[10] This is intersectionality in scholarship.

Male dominance is still the prevailing narrative in the church, removing womanhood from the divine. As previously stated, the Bible is predominantly written by male authors from within a patriarchal society. From this male positionality, the stories of women leaders and benefactors of the early church were omitted or underestimated.[11] Now, through womanist biblical scholarship, we know that women were also benefactors and disciples during Christ's ministry. Women were at his crucifixion, the first at the tomb, and the first to announce and understand his resurrection. God placed the most important message of all time into the mouths of women.[12] During

Paul's time, women were leaders in the early church along with men. As womanist theologian Karen Baker-Fletcher writes:

> Womanist hope is found in that which is greater and stronger than any evil. Such hope transcends fear, creating visions of promise and resource for survival, for resistance against evil, for liberation, and for healing. "The Lord" refers to God, which from a womanist perspective is "Spirit." . . . We are not accustomed to thinking of ourselves as truly created in God's image, which means we have difficulty imagining God as female.[13]

Telling the story of God from a woman's perspective is to tell a counterstory in the language of CRT. Duncan writes, "Just don't be surprised if the Holy Spirit is a Black woman." This spiritual perspective is in line with the spirit of intersectionality.

CRT AND SYSTEMIC SEXISM

Gloria Steinem, a leading American feminist, once named Derrick Bell "an honorary woman, because he was a feminist before feminism was cool."[14] Bell understood that the various forms of oppression are not "divorceable from one another nor amenable to strict categorization."[15] So while CRT mainly engaged systemic racism, it acknowledges that other forms of systemic oppression exist in conjunction with racism: sexism, ageism, classism, ableism, et cetera—intersectionality. Bell understood that students gained from seeing the law through the eyes of women legal experts.

CRT and intersectionality are helpful in analyzing church hierarchy, patriarchal systems, and sexist policies that discriminate in terms of who gets hired, who preaches, who makes decisions, who is heard, and even how God is understood. Church systems and policies that silence and marginalize women impact women's spiritual growth, their identity in Christ, and their participation in ministry.

To be sure, CRT originated in legal studies, and its focus was on policies, institutions, and legal strategies following the civil rights movement. Early CRT theorists never directly addressed the church as an institution, nor was CRT used to analyze systemic policies around women in the church. However, the effectiveness of this theory when applied to systems other than law speaks to it strength.

THE SYSTEMIC SILENCING OF WOMEN

In interviewing women from a variety of racial backgrounds, but predominantly women of color, I've come to realize that there is no one point of view on the church and women, and no one common experience. The women I spoke with hold on to their faith despite their acknowledgment of systems that oppress them. One woman stated that her church was her family—sometimes dysfunctional, but no less her family. Women have been and continue to be the backbone of most churches, whether this is recognized or not. Some women feel alone among the crowd; others acknowledge the inequality of women within their ranks but choose to stay and work within the church. There are as many experiences as there are women, but without exception, they know the church discriminates against them.

This has been my own experience as well. In the spirit of CRT and counter-storytelling, I tell my story of silencing. I am a white woman and recognize my privilege of race, but through an intersectional lens, I also see systems and policies of discrimination toward women in the church. I suspect these experiences are more frequent and acute for Black women.

From the year 2010 onward, I attended an Assembly of God church that was considered an evangelical, interracial, and intercultural church of approximately 1,500 members. Upon meeting women in the church and becoming involved in ministry, I realized that men held all leadership and decision-making positions and that the board of directors was made up of solely men. When attending the yearly congregational business meeting, I saw nominations for new board members were announced; no women were nominated for the twelve or so positions. I was surprised because I knew many professional women who were better-qualified than the men who had been nominated. I heard women whispering in the pew behind me and I turned around, asking, "Why no women?" The women just shook their heads from side to side as if to say, "It's disgusting, isn't it?" The incident disturbed me, as I had been optimistic about this congregation.

I set about the next year talking to pastors, the women's group leaders, church congregants, and administrators. I found that when a list of eligible candidates for the board was submitted for nomination, half of the congregants were omitted—the women. I researched the bylaws of the Assemblies of God national organization, of which this local church was subordinate (General Presbytery, 2010), as well as the scriptures and theological books on the subject. I found no prohibition on women in ministry in the Assemblies of God (General Presbytery, 2010), and a plethora of support for women leaders in the Bible.

Several church leaders suggested that I bring my concern to the next church business meeting during the open mic—a scheduled opportunity for questions, concerns, and suggestions from the congregation. Sensing the audience would be at least somewhat hostile to my position, I prepared a well-thought-out statement, explaining the evidence from Assemblies of God's policies, the scriptures, and my personal experience. I prayed a great deal. I did not know how hostile the audience would be.

The night of the meeting, several hundred members attended. Once again, no women were nominated to the board. I had vowed to God that I would stand up to speak if this were the case. With trepidation, I went to the open mic and began. Early on, the pastor interrupted to ask what I was going to address. I replied, "The nomination of women to the board." He abruptly responded, "Now is not the time, you can speak at the end. We are talking about the budget now." I sat down, realizing just how much opposition there would be. I began to tremble.

At the end of the meeting, as promised, the pastor said, "Joni, now you can speak." This time, without interruption, I delivered my prepared argument. You could have heard a pin drop in the room. I was told later that the pastors on stage behind me had been pacing and appeared agitated.

Finished, I sat down. The pastor was visibly angry, saying, "Does anyone have anything to say?" Complete silence. Even those who had promised to support my position were silent—not that I blamed them. The pastor looked furious. He then exclaimed, "That was out of order!" I do not remember anything more, only that I felt like someone had punched me in the chest. I loved the church, the people, and the pastor, which is why I even thought to protest this injustice. To the pastor and church's credit, a few years later, women were nominated to the board. Many years later, one woman was elected.

The silencing of women is accomplished through verbal and public assaults like this, and also through microaggressions, omissions, and erasures. This silencing may be another reason why churches seem to be losing their young congregants. Young women today know "too much." I will never forget this experience, and when one has had enough of being silenced, the words of Father Bryan Massingale ring very true:

> Why do I keep doing what I am doing for a church that would be more comforted by my absence and silence? A church that would be happier if I just walked away? A church that probably would not even miss my presence or contributions? All of this effort and for what?[16]

Massingale's answer to his own question is that he does not have a choice. God called him to speak, to engage, to resist, to challenge, to not remain silent.[17] I concur. My resistance and protest was tiny in comparison to thousands of others who have lost employment, citizenship, and opportunities when confronting injustice. And yet, we each in our corner of the world are called by God to confront injustice where we find it. We may be silenced, yet we must speak.

OTHER INTERSECTIONALITIES

CRT and intersectionality in its original formation dealt predominantly with the intersection of race and gender. Today, however, intersectionality is applied to diverse fields of study, including public health, criminal justice, LGBTQ studies, and disability studies. CRT is the target of most conservative arguments, but there is a huge field of related study. One of those offshoots is DisCrit, a combination of disability studies and CRT. This field of study looks at how racism and ableism operate together, analyzing cultural, historical, relational, social, and political aspects of the disabled.[18]

An undergraduate student of mine wrote an autoethnographic research paper that explored his deafness and his identity as a young Black male. His paper explored how his difficult interactions with police were exacerbated by both racial stereotyping and his inability to hear when police officers spoke to him. Police officers and other authorities often thought he was being disrespectful or uncooperative when he could not hear them. This resulted in several unreasonable arrests. His race and disability interconnected, thereby increasing the potential for discrimination by police. This kind of experience is a prime focus of DisCrit studies. For human services professionals and scholars of all sorts, the intersectional perspective provides a nuanced and accurate analysis of discrimination within their fields. DisCrit is but one example.

WHY IT MATTERS FOR THE CHURCH

Intersectionality is a powerful tool in understanding policies, institutions, and people in nuanced ways, and it also helps us to see the world through the eyes of others. It can combat injustice. The prophet Micah declared, "He has shown you, O man, what is good; and what does the Lord require of you, but to do justly, to love mercy, and to walk humbly with your God."[19] It is hard to argue that justice, love, and humility toward God and our fellow man are not pillars of the

Christian faith. In addition, justice for the poor and marginalized is a particular theme throughout the scriptures. Therefore, churches need to address injustice; it is the church's calling and responsibility. The church should be leading the way; however, this does not seem to be the case. Among conservative churches, there is what political scientists call "dominant group status threat," a fear by men and white people that their status within the hierarchy is threatened. This harkens to "take our country back" and "make America great again."[20] This kind of fear is not of God.[21] This fearful malaise does not bode well for the mental health of church members or the health of the church.

The American church as an institution has little creditability because it has not in any consistent and pervasive way engaged a critical faith. This is perhaps one of the reasons young people are leaving the church from all denominations, and why some churches avoid the label *evangelical*.[22] In the last decade, that term has become associated with intolerance, racism, homophobia, sexism, ignorance, right-wing politics, and conspiracy theories. White evangelicals are the religious group most opposed to vaccines, most convinced that the 2020 presidential election was fraudulent, and most likely to espouse the QAnon conspiracy. Evangelicals are infighting, have become compulsively political, and have been reduced to caricature.[23] As journalist Tim Alberta states, "This is heartbreaking." This is particularly true for those of us who profess Christ and love the church.

CRT and intersectionality are misunderstood words that are sure to rile up emotions. But these theories can help churches respond to God's calling to do justice, love mercy, and walk humbly with our God.

NOTES

1 PBS, "Sojourner Truth."
2 Kennedy, "Voting Rights."
3 PBS, "Sojourner Truth."
4 Crenshaw, "Essential Reading."

5 African American Policy Forum, "A Primer."
6 Strachan and MacArthur, *Christianity and Wokeness*.
7 Cone, *Black Theology & Black Power*.
8 Walker, *In Search*.
9 McCaulley, *Reading While Black*.
10 Brown, *Blackening of the Bible*; Lovelace, "Womanist Biblical Interpretation."
11 Duncan, *Dear Church*; Malcolm, *Women at the Crossroads*.
12 Kroeger, "The Neglected History."
13 Baker-Fletcher, *Sisters of Dust, Sisters of Spirit*.
14 Christopher, "Derrick Bell's Widow."
15 Bell, *Faces at the Bottom*.
16 Massingale, *Racial Justice and the Catholic Church*.
17 Massingale, "Black Faith Matters: Harlem."
18 Annamma, Ferri, and Connor, "Disability Critical Race Theory."
19 Mi 6:8 (New King James Version).
20 Wilkerson, *Caste*.
21 1 Jn 4:18 (NIV).
22 Nadeem, "Modeling the Future."
23 Alberta, "How Politics Poisoned."

CHAPTER ELEVEN

No White Saviors
Faith and White Allies

"If you are neutral in a situation of injustice, you have chosen the side of the oppressor. If an elephant has his foot on the tail of the mouse, and you say you are neutral, the mouse will not appreciate your neutrality."

—Desmond Tutu[1]

There is no neutrality to faith or justice.[2] And CRT does take a side. As a cross-disciplinary theory, it is used by civil rights activist scholars with the goal of societal change. The *critical* in CRT and critical faith is about critical thinking and the scholarly critique that leads to action.

To be both a Christian and an anti-racist is to take sides—the side of the poor, oppressed, and disenfranchised. There is no middle ground, no in-between. There are perpetrators, bystanders, and activists.[3] You cannot be passive in this conversation. Anti-racism is a decision, a commitment, a passion, and a response to God's call. It is a life's journey.

This chapter begins with a discussion of white anti-racist allies, focusing on the scholarship of Ibram X. Kendi, and the life of Dietrich Bonhoeffer. Many contemporary and historical white anti-racist allies could have been chosen for consideration: Tim Wise, Abigail Hopper-Gibbons, Jim Wallis, Drick Boyd, Myles Horton, Angelina Grimké, and Robert P. Jones, to name a few.[4] I chose Dietrich Bonhoeffer, a Christian scholar and martyr, because of his life-altering connection to a Black church, community, and theology.

ANTI-RACIST AND WHITE ALLIES

Ibram X. Kendi's books are banned in some schools, and his name is linked to CRT, although he is not a CRT scholar. Kendi was born Ibram Henry Rogers in 1982 of parents who came of age during the Black Power movement in New York City. They were activist Christians inspired by Black liberation theology. Today both of Kendi's parents are Methodist ministers with strong liberation theology roots. Kendi has been described by his wife as influenced by the faith and activism of his parents: "When he [Kendi] speaks, I can hear the Black church come out. You can tell he's a preacher's kid. . . . He's not really preaching, but he sounds like it sometimes."[5]

"I cannot disconnect my parents' religious strivings to be Christian from my secular strivings to be an antiracist," he writes.[6] Indeed, Christianity and anti-racism were intimately connected for his parents. They were inspired by Tom Skinner, a fiery Black evangelist who preached the Gospel of "Jesus Christ the Radical," and by James H. Cone, one of the originators of Black liberation theology. Kendi's parents taught him Black pride, and he took these lessons seriously. As Kendi tells it, his parents' beliefs and example led him to embrace Black self-reliance, a doctrine that urged Black people to overcome the legacy of racism by working hard and doing well.[7]

Christianity and anti-racism are deeply connected. Anti-racism is an outgrowth of faith in Christ. For Kendi, a public intellectual, there is no neutrality; he wants to tell the truth and to clarify for all peoples through his scholarship and writing what anti-racism is. Anti-racism is the practice or policy of opposing racism and promoting racial equity. From a CRT lens, *institutional racism, structural racism* and *systemic racism* are redundant because racism is all three: structural, systemic, and institutional. Then it follows, an anti-racist is anyone (of any race) who supports anti-racist policy through their words and deeds. Inherent in this definition is the understanding that inaction or silence is neutral and that neutrality is racist.[8]

It bears repeating that Kendi does not consider himself a CRT scholar, but his definition of anti-racism is consistent with CRT. CRT is an activist theory with the ultimate goal of challenging ideologies that limit the understanding of racism to interpersonal behaviors and to instead work toward structural change. All peoples are needed to achieve these goals, and this chapter focuses on white allies. According to Boyd, white anti-racist allies are those who assume a "positive white identity based on reality, not on assumed priority, white privilege, or superiority," but rather align themselves with people of color in seeking to bring about racial justice.[9]

In spiritual terms, Jeremiah 22:13–17 sums up what it is to be a Christian and anti-racist in the context of America: It is to know God and to be an ally of both God and humanity. According to Jeremiah, to know God is to do justice by the poor, marginalized, and oppressed, and to break with systems of tyranny, inequity, and inequality.[10] Many theologians and writers address the Bible's preferential emphasis on the poor. Overwhelmingly, authors of the Bible reference the weak and oppressed more than other groups of people.[11] Jesus gave preference to the poor in his parables, in associations and friendships, and in what he resisted. But as has been mentioned, the church historically and contemporaneously spiritualizes the poor to mean "the poor or weak in spirit," rather than focusing on socioeconomics. This is an incomplete reading of the scriptures.[12] The anti-racist ally understands the scriptures to mean that *poor* can mean spiritually or economically, in particular, those groups who experience injustice by way of unjust policies, laws, ideologies, traditions, and bureaucracies. The white anti-racist ally is in solidarity with people of color.

God uses such people and brings about his judgment of corrupt institutions through human agency.[13] This necessitates resistance to and criticism of the status quo. In the current debate, it means a criticism of America and its history. For some opponents of CRT, criticizing America is somehow perceived as being disloyal or unpatriotic. On the contrary, just as Nathan the prophet confronted and criticized David for his affair with Bathsheba and murder of Uriah, her husband, those who criticize do so out of love. The willingness to confront, grapple with, and—yes—criticize America is to love her.[14]

To be a white anti-racist ally is to suffer with and to risk. We serve a risk-taking God. The risks include being misunderstood, disliked and labeled, subjected to physical violence and emotional trauma, experiencing violence to property or harm to reputation, and dismissal or erasure. There are also pitfalls to the sometimes dangerous business of being a white anti-racist ally in the forms of paternalism, interest convergence, and colorblindness. Undoubtedly, the risks and costs for white anti-racist allies are far less than those for people of color. The cost for Kendi has been his body's response to his anti-racist research. He wonders sometimes whether his battle with cancer might be due to the intense and traumatic nature of his work.[15]

THE COST OF ANTI-RACISM

For Dietrich Bonhoeffer, the cost was death. He was martyred for his opposition to the Nazis and the complicit German church. A German Lutheran pastor, Bonhoeffer was one of the founders of the Confessing Church—one of the only churches in Germany to stand up to Nazism and antisemitism in Hitler's Germany.

But Bonhoeffer was not always opposed to Hitler's Germany. He started out as a staunch supporter of nationalism and claimed theological justification for national domination of the German people, a pure race, and the exploitation of the other—Jews, Roma, the disabled, and homosexuals.[16] The Reich's political ideology, when mixed with the theology of the German Christian movement, turned Jesus into a divine representation of the so-called pure Aryan and allowed race-hate to become part of Germany's religious life. The church supported a white supremacist German-centered mentality that held the Aryan race to be superior to all others. It is hard not to compare the contemporary rhetoric of American exceptionalism to the German ideology of the 1930s pre–World War II. This is the Germany that Bonhoeffer grew up in, and the German nationalism that was linked closely with Christianity.[17]

LEARNING FROM THE BLACK CHURCH IN HARLEM

But then there was Harlem. Bonhoeffer, as a twenty-four-year-old postdoctoral student, spent 1930–1931 at Union Theological Seminary in New York, making a second trip in 1939. That year in New York changed Bonhoeffer from an academic nationalist theologian to a passionate follower of Christ. He would return to Germany transformed to become a brave Christian leader and martyr, standing against Hitler and the mainstream German church, and later dying in a concentration camp.[18]

His conversion did not take place at the seminary where he studied, in the white church, or with a white Jesus. Bonhoeffer found the Black Jesus of the Harlem Renaissance and the Christianity that later propelled the civil rights movement. He found his faith at Abyssinian Baptist Church under the leadership of Adam Clayton Powell Sr. The people of Harlem taught him empathy and co-suffering with the poor and oppressed. He met a Jesus who suffered at the hands of injustice. He learned from the African American community that the white Jesus was a problem who instigated Black oppression. Black Christians and theology led him to his calling to return to Germany to suffer and fight for the outcasts and scapegoats who were being exterminated.[19] In Harlem, Dietrich had a newfound understanding of what it meant to be a Christian and embraced a Jesus who stood with the oppressed rather than join the oppressors. His theology challenged the way God embodies race and religion.

Bonhoeffer's Black Jesus argues that obedience requires concrete action. There is occasion for the ethic of resistance, not only in

Harlem and the German church in the 1930s, but in the American church today. Bonhoeffer was indebted to the Black church for his conversion and political activism. At great cost, Bonhoeffer became an anti-racist ally and one of the most impactful theologians of the twentieth century.

PATERNALISM AND PATRONIZING—WHAT ANTI-RACISM IS NOT

Now to clarify what anti-racism is not: It is not individual charity, it is not pity, it is not guilt, and it is not patronizing. *Paternalism* is the quality of acting like a father or mother, while *patronizing* is being offensively condescending; I will use them interchangeably. I have seen paternalism up close in an evangelical megachurch. Behind closed doors, some members of the mostly non-white congregation called the church "the plantation." Run like a plantation, white "overseers" exercised the power of the budget, the decision-making, and the authority to promote and demote. Black and Hispanic men were given roles as associate pastors with little power, authority, or privilege. Women, in particular Black and Hispanic women, functioned as administrative staff under a hierarchical leadership, carrying the bulk of administrative work under a strict chain of command. Control of communication, resources, and ministries ultimately came from the lead white pastor.

The problem is that this leadership is patronizing and sometimes infantilizing. There was the illusion that the assistant pastors of color had power, but they had a title with little ability to exercise it. Any power they did possess was not infrequently undermined by the white leadership. Members of the congregation tithed and gave offerings regularly but with no transparency to see where the money was spent. There was no representative voice on a board of directors or advisory council to give input. The congregation and staff were often treated like children, and some resented this but were afraid to speak up for fear of reprisal.

This church was interracial but not anti-racist. Unfortunately, I saw this example repeated in other churches. Ministry and missions were viewed by the institution as "doing some good in the hood" or "helping those poor people." From the white leadership there appeared little comprehension of Watson's quote, "If you have come here to help me, then you are wasting your time, but if you have come because your liberation is bound up in mine, then let us work together."[20]

Reciprocity of relationship, especially across race, was missing. Equity and shared leadership were foreign terms. Any racial problems were framed as urban and minority problems. The idea that white supremacy and white people were the problem could not be conceived. James Baldwin explained this ignorance: "The confusion in this country that we call the Negro problem has nothing to do with Negroes."[21] There is no Black problem but a white problem—everyone's problem. Unless we realize this, we will never move forward.

With paternalism often comes a culture where criticism is not only discouraged but punished. You can lose your job or be demoted, ostracized, and verbally abused for criticizing the church, especially regarding racial issues. In these oppressive church cultures, Black people learn to perform. Lucas on this phenomenon in the Catholic Church:

> Dishonesty and deceit are so often a part of black/white communication. . . . We said one thing among ourselves and as soon as the man appeared, we showed our teeth and told him what he wanted to hear. Black people in this country are experts on surviving.[22]

Patronizing in the Catholic Church mirrors what goes on in Protestant circles: "The process is that the man chooses black leadership for black people on the basis of whom he considers a Tom."[23] These are often not adult-to-adult relationships but rather paternalistic relationships. Often there is kindness until the white priest or pastor is crossed, criticized, or confronted as an equal. According to Lucas:

> It is not his kindness that is at fault but a deep-rooted inability to deal with a [Black person] on any level other than the [Black person] being in some need, the Black's begging or requesting something he is able to bestow . . . The Black's need of him [the White man], whether it be the social, intellectual, or economic order, is the basis of the relationship . . . The superior white man doles out patronage out of largess to the inferior POC.
>
> Lucas, 1990, p. 215

This is a white savior complex. This rescuing and patronage is not ministry. Genuine love between white people and Black people cannot exist apart from freedom, equality, and justice for Black people in and outside the church. Priests, pastors, and ministers have to move from their historically and psychologically conditioned role of father and mother, beyond paternalism and the white savior complex.[24]

INTEREST CONVERGENCE

The term *interest convergence* originated with CRT and posited that substantive legal gains for racial minorities usually do not occur unless they benefit or converge with the interests of whites. This concept has been referred to and briefly defined previously. As related to the church, Duncan frames interest convergence this way:

> I have the same realization that I have often had at synod assemblies or at the seminary. . . . that I am loved by this church as a black person only when we serve its agenda . . . [T]he white church loves us only when we fit its current worldview or goals.[25]

Derrick Bell introduced the concept in the 1980s in his widely read *Harvard Law Review* comments about Brown v. Board of Education, arguing that the passage of Brown gave elite whites and the US credibility in communist-leaning countries, while boosting US prestige toward economic advantages at home. (For an in-depth understanding of Bell's argument, see Bell, 1980.) Suffice it to say that interest convergence in part explains why the desegregation of schools has still not become a reality. We are just as segregated now as in the 1950s.[26] The legislation dismantled Black schools, left many Black teachers unemployed, and left many schools still segregated and unequal. In other words, societal change designed to make life equitable for minorities sometimes makes the situation worse, further oppressing the groups intended to be liberated.

A disclaimer is needed in regards to individual as contrasted to group interest convergence. While Bell and most CRT theorists use the term to represent group action which can have both positive and negative results, I am applying the term to individual and group action, as the theory has been expanded beyond Bell's original concept.[27] In the opening of this book, I broach my own awareness and struggle with interest convergence as it relates to a white woman writing about race in America. I understand this to be individual interest convergence.

This also applies in church organizations. Interest convergence can happen when white people think they are doing good. For example, bringing in Black speakers or musicians to white or interracial churches can be wonderful, but can also be in the self-interest of white people. It can be in the service of interest convergence when the prevailing attitude is "look how interracial we are." Some white leaders use people of color to prop up their ministries, using their testimonies to raise money for their own church, all in the name of helping "those poor people." Mission trips can exhibit the white savior syndrome, undermining local cultural and ethnic strengths while satisfying white people's desire to feel needed.

For some, the Southern Baptist Conference's June 1995 decision to reverse its position on race could either be seen as interest convergence or divine inspiration. This reversal included an apology to African Americans for slavery, Jim Crow, and their lack of support during the civil rights movement. As no reparations were given, this decision could be too late and too small a response. For some it smacks of interest convergence, a bowing to political pressure and shrinking church membership rather than authentic repentance.[28]

Churches are notorious for marketing that they are diverse while white people hold control; white supremacy is still alive. Church bulletins, advertising, and websites often photograph a church's few Black members to make the church appear inclusive. This is interest convergence at the expense of reality. The opposite of interest convergence is in Bell's words the courage to avoid self-interest:

> Courage is a decision you make to act in a way that works through your own fear for the greater good as opposed to pure self-interest. Courage means putting at risk your immediate self-interest for what you believe is right.[29]

The possibility of interest convergence is always present. Very few of us act in ways that are completely selfless. Therefore, we need to listen and reflect on our movements, agency, and positionality within churches to change the institution at the root and avoid replicating patterns of behavior that meet our own ends. We need to examine what it means to be anti-racist within church structures, not only when it is of benefit to increase church membership, fundraise, sell books, or appear politically correct.

COLORBLINDNESS

"The heartbeat of racism is denial, and really the heartbeat of anti-racism is confession."[30] Churches are notorious for colorblind rhetoric. You frequently hear, "We are all one, there is no racism here," "I don't see color; I just see people," "I don't care if you are Black, white, red, blue, or purple," "all lives matter," and "I have Black friends." Colorblindness is the unwillingness or inability to acknowledge that social constructs of race exist and impact equitable life outcomes.

Colorblindness implies that racism does not exist so long as you ignore it. It serves as a dismissal of the lived experiences of people of color and is a way to avoid conversations about race and racism.[31] The term *blind* in this context means the refusal to see difference or grapple with inequities. A colorblind perspective ignores structural racism and keeps the status quo, thereby shutting one's eyes to racism in the everyday life of the church. The church is notorious for this approach.

I recall a conversation with a white pastor who, when confronted with the notion that, by virtue of being white in America, he possessed white privilege, could not accept this. The pastor became noticeably uncomfortable, denying that he had any privilege whatsoever. He communicated that he was not elitist and was the same as everyone one else. His refusal to entertain the possibility that his race gave him advantage is an example of colorblindness. Another white pastor, when asked to think about his white privilege as he was ministering in a predominantly Black, multiethnic church, shut this possibility down because God had given him a special calling to minister to Black people. It hurt him to think it might have been his own unearned white privilege that contributed to his successful ministry.

I have mixed feelings about calling churches *multiethnic* and not *multiracial*. It is true the term *multiethnic* is empirically more accurate, but the omission of the term *multiracial* may be less a product of scientific accuracy and more a move to avoid the conversation of race. Suffice to say, white anti-racist allies must learn to be comfortable talking about racism, confronting the structures that uphold it, and being proactive in identifying racism. CRT is a threat to colorblindness because it challenges the status quo and promotes difficult dialogues. Colorblindness is neither anti-racism nor in the service of white allies.

INTERRACIAL RELATIONSHIPS

Black people marrying white people, white families adopting Black children, and white people having a Black pastor or associate pastor do not erase white privilege or change systemic racism. Sadly, not even Vice President Kamala Harris and Supreme Court Justice Ketanji Brown Jackson having white husbands means that systemic racism has ended. Having Black friends does not make a white person an anti-racist ally. Likewise, calling one's church "interracial" does not mean that systems of racism are not operative.[32]

The definition most often used for a multiethnic church (which seems to be the term now used instead of *interracial)* is a church where no one ethnicity makes up more than 80 percent of the congregation.[33] It is true that multiracial churches—and this is hopeful news—have increased in the past twenty years, but sheer numbers do not tell the whole story. Research on interracial churches reports that the same inequities that pervade society also plague interracial and multiethnic churches. These inequities include individualistic white ideas of race (no application of a CRT lens), leaders of color with no power, people of color delegated to symbolic roles (usher, singer, maintenance, hospitality aide, etc.), and race and racism never being discussed from the pulpit.[34]

No doubt, interracial relationships are good and have the potential to make individuals anti-racist allies, but not necessarily so. Much depends upon the quality of and equality in those relationships.

EMBRACING A WHITE ANTI-RACIST
STANCE—WHERE TO BEGIN

To be a white anti-racist ally is to be passionate about racial justice and to act in your corner of the world to move it forward. These are individuals who understand CRT (even if he or she does not use that label).

To be a white anti-racist ally is to be afraid, anxious, but brave; it is to say "yes" to life and the spirit. To be an anti-racist ally is to engage in a life that seeks to understand the pervasive nature of the struggle within the lives of most Black people.[35] It is a life of passion for racial justice. It is listening to the call of Jesus to be present in America's current struggles.

One of the most damning but accurate reports on racism in the church is *"Brothers and Sisters to Us,"* a 1979 US Catholic Bishops' pastoral letter to the church.[36] It reads like the religious version of the 1968 Kerner Commission Report issued by the congressional committee established by President Johnson to examine race and poverty.[37] Both reports are comprehensive, accurate, and identify structural issues supporting racism. Both reports identify structural racism and racial bias. To work toward racial justice in the church and society could begin with a good read of both reports. When it comes to issues of racial justice, we know what to do; the question is, Do we as a nation and church have the will to do it?

And then white allies must do as Bonhoeffer did and learn from Black brothers and sisters. Bonhoeffer was transformed by the preaching of Adam Clayton Powell Sr. and Albert Fisher, a fellow scholar and friend from Harlem. Bonhoeffer listened, watched, and learned. He was taught that social and political action on behalf of the oppressed and poor is a sacred core of Christian responsibility. He learned that Christian discipleship includes a this-world pursuit of justice, and that spirituality is both individualistic and collective.

In Harlem he learned a holistic engagement with the sacred in everyday life. He learned that a solely spiritualized gospel is a mockery of faith and an opiate of the people. From Powell he learned that "faithful stewardship of God's resources requires recognizing the pre-eminence of Christ and that, in obedience to Christ, God's people are called to action to relieve suffering."[38] In Harlem, he was taught Christ-centered resistance to wrongs.

As a writer, anti-racist scholar, and Christian, I am not much in favor of easy how-to's or laundry lists of "how to become." Yet in this instance, perhaps a list of what I wish church leaders would have told me early on during my Christian journey and ministry may be helpful to someone seeking a critical faith that embraces an anti-racist stance:

1. Listen to people of color and understand critical race theory
2. Read banned books (they are banned because they challenge you to think critically); the "Brothers and Sisters to Us" and Kerner reports; and books on Black theology
3. Pray for racial justice in yourself and the church
4. Show preference for and focus on the poor and oppressed
5. Examine your white privilege, interest convergence, and colorblindness; confess racism individually and collectively
6. Learn to be comfortable discussing race in multiracial settings; be a boundary crosser (spanning race, ethnicity, and class)
7. Risk being wrong and admit when you are
8. Be brave, relying on the Holy Spirit; develop Christ-centered resistance; tackle structural racism in society and the church
9. Express regret (without personal guilt) for ancestral wrongs
10. Consider supporting reparations for Black churches and communities
11. Support Black leadership and churches led by leadership of color
12. Love Jesus in and through the racial divide and listen to the Holy Spirit in going forward

We are in this together. The issue of racial justice touches all Christians and Americans. It is everyone's issue. We are all harmed, are made less than, and have been wounded by racism, whether we realize it or not. Duncan, in his courageous letter to the white church, captures the cost (think Bonhoeffer) and what is at stake:

> To actively work with me in lockstep to bring justice and equity to my people—that's going to cost you. That may cost you

everything. You may have to lay aside years of beliefs and practices. You may have to give up your very grip on world history and your place in it. You may have to share or give up real power. Yet it's not just my freedom you are risking it all for, but also your own. You are just as trapped by the effects of chattel slavery and the broken cycles it has set in motion on our nation and church.[39]

The white anti-racist comprehends white privilege as "a fatal privilege," as Bonhoeffer saw the insidious ethnic pride and Aryan privilege of the Nazis, and "cannot claim to know Christ and ignore injustice."[40] The white anti-racist ally is a burden-bearer, someone with "a view from below."[41] Bonhoeffer's view from below parallels CRT's "faces at the bottom" and "bottom inquiry."[42] The white Christian anti-racist ally sees Christ hidden in suffering and racial marginalization and acts on that perspective. Amen and amen, Church.

NOTES

1 Labbé-DeBose, "Black Women."
2 Kendi, *Stamped*.
3 Gushee, *Still Christian*.
4 Boyd and Vivian, *White Allies*.
5 Sanneh, "The Fight to Redefine Racism."
6 Kendi, *How to Be an Antiracist*.
7 Sanneh, "The Fight to Redefine Racism."
8 Kendi, *Stamped*.
9 Boyd and Vivian, *White Allies*.
10 Brown, *Unexpected News*.
11 Brown.
12 Brown; Massingale, *Racial Justice and the Catholic Church*; McCaulley, *Reading While Black*; Cone, *Black Theology & Black Power*.
13 McCaulley, *Reading While Black*.
14 Brown, *Unexpected News*.
15 Talesnik, "Kendi Expounds."
16 Williams, *Bonhoeffer's Black Jesus*.
17 Williams.

18 Bonhoeffer and Metaxas, *The Cost of Discipleship*.
19 Williams, *Bonhoeffer's Black Jesus*.
20 Baldwin, *The Cross of Redemption*.
21 Baldwin, *The Cross of Redemption*.
22 Lucas, *Black Priest White Church*.
23 Lucas.
24 Lucas.
25 Duncan, *Dear Church*.
26 Breyer and Vignarajah, *Breaking the Promise*.
27 Morrison, "Whose Interests and Under Whose Control?"
28 Blumenfeld, "Interest Convergence."
29 Bell, *Ethical Ambition*.
30 Kendi, "There Is No Debate."
31 Emerson, "Mosaix Global Newsletter"; Maurice Asare, "Debunking."
32 Touré, "No, Newsmax."
33 Edwards, "The Multiethnic Church."
34 Edwards.
35 Massingale, *Racial Justice and the Catholic Church*.
36 USCCB, "Brothers and Sisters."
37 Cobb and Guariglia, *The Essential Kerner*.
38 Williams, *Bonhoeffer's Black Jesus*.
39 Duncan, *Dear Church*.
40 Williams, *Bonhoeffer's Black Jesus*.
41 Williams.
42 Williams; Matsuda, "Looking to the Bottom."

CHAPTER TWELVE

The Lynching Tree
and the Cross

> "The cross helped me to deal with the brutal legacy of the lynching tree, and the lynching tree helped me to understand the tragic meaning of the cross."[1]
>
> —James H. Cone

Lynching is the history that America does not want to tell. Between 1880 and 1940, white Christians lynched nearly five thousand Black men and women. This was domestic terrorism. In some instances, the event of spectacle lynching was announced in churches and viewed by churchgoers after services. Jesus's crucifixion was a first-century lynching and public spectacle meant to warn Roman subjects not to engage in sedition or criticism of the empire. American lynching sanctioned by white authorities sent a message to Black people to stay in their place, stay away from white women, and obey Jim Crow.

The cross on Golgotha and the lynching tree ought to find a prominent place in American Christianity because the similarities are as frightening as they are self-evident. But the connection is practically absent from sermons, theological writing, and religious imagery, at least in white theological thought.

THEORY AND THEOLOGY—WHITE
THEOLOGY AND RACE

Theory is not theology, and theory is not a religion or cult. Theory comes from the ancient Greek *theoria*, meaning to contemplate, look at, and examine. Whereas theology comes from the Greek *theos*, meaning God, and *logia*, thinking or studying. Although similar in etymology, they are distinct. Theology interprets the scriptures from two social locations: the positionality of the theologian and the social context, culture, and the intentions of the Bible's authors. God's word to man is communicated within the Bible's history and culture to the readers' history and culture, then applied to the current personal and social context of the believer. To argue otherwise is to hold a traditional belief that there is only one way to interpret scripture—literally. Good biblical theology interprets the scripture in totality by analyzing the overall themes, topics, and messages that pervade the Old and New Testaments and applying them to the context in which people live. In America, theology is racialized—white and Black theology. During Jim Crow, white theology ignored the application of faith to the extrajudicial violent torture, hanging, mutilation, decapitation, and burning alive of victims that marked the collective sin of lynching.

White theologians, predominantly white men, study the Bible from the benefit of the dominant culture. Their social location as white men, therefore, informs America's understanding of race and gender within the Bible. One of the most renowned white theologians was Reinhold Niebuhr (1892–1971). His prolific writings on the cross and Jesus's suffering lived vicariously by Christians are the crux of white theology. And yet, not even Niebuhr understood that the most obvious cross-bearers in America were Black people, whose lynchings were scattered across the country. Niebuhr was a gradualist and supported moderate Southerners on integration, opposing protest and violence in response to racial oppression.[2] His stance is representative of the white pastors' pleas to Martin Luther King to move slowly in the face of racial injustice.

Historically, white theology propped up the institution of slavery and supported slave owners' cruelty.

Douglass's master was converted and became more vicious than before his conversion. It was as if the slaveholder now had the church to justify his behavior:

The man who wields the blood-clotted cowskin during the week
fills the pulpit on Sunday, and claims to be a minister of the
meek and lowly Jesus. The man who robs me of my earnings
at the end of each week meets me as a class-leader on Sunday
morning, to show me the way of life, and the path of salvation.
He who sells my sister, for purposes of prostitution, stands forth
as the pious advocate of purity. He who proclaims it a religious
duty to read the Bible denies me the right of learning to read
the name of God who made me.[3]

Slave owners presented Christianity and Christ to Black slaves in order to save their souls and keep them submissive. Owners mutilated the Bible, giving slaves only parts of the scriptures, the slave Bible. Certain parts were cut out; Exodus was revised so as not to give the slaves ideas about rebellion, enmeshing the Bible and American Protectionism.[4] Yet Black people saw in both the Old and New Testament liberation from physical slavery. Slaveholders were threatened by the scriptures because they confronted their privilege and justification to own slaves. Both slaves and slaveholders brought their concerns to the scriptures. Slaveholders read from their lust for power and wealth, and slaves from a position of oppression and resistance—the same scripture with vastly different interpretations. Black people "did not locate the problem with the scriptures themselves, but rather with the interpretation of these texts."[5]

American slavery as an institution is abolished, while institutional racism continues. Yet the Gospel that saves the soul but leaves out liberation for the poor and oppressed is still prevalent in white and interracial churches.[6] Sadly, in the twenty-first century, white theological perspectives either continue to prop up or remain silent about racial injustice, as Niebuhr did during the civil rights movement. At that time, the majority of white churches were absent in opposing desegregation, participating in nonviolent protests, or supporting Martin Luther King. The white church was absent from bus boycotts, silent to abusive FBI surveillance, and silent after the murders of Medgar Evers, Malcolm X, Fred Hampton and Mark Clark. The church was silent after the murders of the four little girls in the Little Rock church.

Today there is a failure to interpret scripture in light of the Black Lives Matter movement, George Floyd's murder, and white nationalism; once again there is silence or opposition from pulpits and Christian leaders.

"White theology neglects the subjects of race and white supremacy as applicable to Christian responsibility and ethical engagement."[7] White theology fails to address racial injustice and how whiteness, as social and identity formation and racist systemic practice, works inside and outside the church. Even well-meaning white pastors and progressive white theologians are impacted by a theology that focuses on individual salvation at the neglect of collective engagement in racial justice.[8] In this failure to examine white supremacy and white privilege, the church becomes at best impotent and at worst complicit in the current racial struggles in this country. To be the "salt of the earth," the church must identify its historical and contemporaneous roots in white supremacy, then work to address it. Unless the church is willing to do this, "Christianity in the West faces a crisis of moral authority."[9] From the framework of CRT, Black liberation theology is the counter to dominant white theology.

THE ERASURE OF BLACK THEOLOGY

Liberation theology and Black liberation theology are related but have different focuses. Both are based on Christian doctrine and are liberationist, seeing social justice as integral to achieving an understanding of the Bible and Jesus. The difference is that Black theology arises from the Black experience in the United States and focuses on the Black community and the Exodus story—God's intervention and liberation of the Jews from slavery in Egypt. The foundational writings for Black theology are James H. Cone's *Black Theology and Black Power* and *A Black Theology of Liberation*. Both assume that biblical texts are read in terms of historical, theological, literary, social, and applicative contexts.[10]

Within the hierarchy of the Catholic Church, liberation theology and Black theology were and sometimes still are threatening.[11] This is also true of evangelical and conservative Protestant churches. Black theology challenges the positionality of the reader and questions the intent of the scriptures. While Black theology does not negate the power of the individual salvation of souls, conversion experiences, or the born-again phenomenon, it recognizes the power of the Gospel to transform both individuals and societal systems. Black theology concurs with white theology: The Bible, with its sixty-six books and 1,189 chapters written, edited, and translated over more than a millennium, is still the inspired word of God.[12] Both Black and white theology locate Jesus as the central figure; Jesus is called the "faithful witness" (Revelation 1:4b–5a), faithful in presenting what God wants to reveal about himself.

And Black theology says that Jesus reveals God as an identifier with the poor and oppressed, as a God who understands living in an oppressed and despised group, a God who experienced violence, who does not uncritically submit to those in power, and who is a liberator of individual souls and marginalized peoples. Black theology understands Jesus to be a subversive and a friend of people who do not belong—critical of systems of power and a threat to the status quo.

Black theology embraces the non-compartmentalizing of Jesus's life—the religious is not separated from the political. Enslaved Black people embraced personal salvation as well as resistance, and this legacy of Black theology continues today. "The early Black churches' reorientation of the Gospel to a more holistic and faithful witness than the one on offer by slave holders is a manifestation of this ongoing conversation about the nature of Christian faith."[13]

Formal Black academic study of the Bible did not begin in earnest until the middle of the twentieth century due to institutionalized racism; however, the integrated approach to theology was born out of the experience of slavery. The theme is God acting to liberate the oppressed and humbling the powerful with "the future of history belonging to the poor and exploited. True liberation will be the work of the oppressed themselves; in them, the Lord saves history."[14] This is the thrust of both liberation theology and Black theology; white theology has no such thrust. A significant strand of the Black Christian tradition and Black theology combines the transformation of systems with the individual transformation of life, while traditional white theology bifurcates them. Jesus's life and ministry embodied the call for liberation and concern for the marginalized.[15] Therefore, worship and prayer are not separated from action and politics. "This bifocal appropriation of the Christian message as a power that can bring about personal and societal change is the Black Christian tradition's gift to the American church."[16]

Yet, I never received this gift. In the forty-eight years since my conversion to Christ, I do not remember a single sermon on racial justice, and I have heard hundreds of sermons. Belonging to multi-racial churches, I was never exposed to great Black theologians like James H. Cone, Howard Thurman, Richard Allen—much less to any liberation theology. Amos, one of the Jewish prophets who exhorted Israel not to forget its commitment to justice, was seldom preached.[17] I was told that the social gospel was not Christ-centered and that Black churches were too socially active. There was an erasure of any Black ecclesial interpretation, with issues of racism and systemic injustice being downplayed.

Despite my years of employment and active participation in the church, Black theology was only broached during my independent study. In several instances, I was called an "old hippie" because I sought to engage social justice concerns with Christianity. I realize now that I was not alone. Seminaries, Christian colleges, and Bible colleges almost never teach Black theology. The bulk of the readings are from white authors taught by predominantly white male professors with the underlying message that these are the only important thinkers.[18] This erasure is a macroaggression and robs everyone of an opportunity to take personal responsibility. It also prevents people from holding their churches accountable in light of injustice.[19] Finally, it dismisses the Black contribution to theology:

> The more time I spent among evangelicals, the more I realized that those spaces can subtly and not subtly breed a certain disdain for what they see as the "uncouthness" of Black culture. We were told that our churches weren't sound theologically because our clergy did not always speak the language of the academy.... It seemed that whatever was going on among Black Christians had little to do with real biblical interpretation. I swam in this disdain, and even when I rejected it vocally, the doubt seeped into my subconscious.[20]

This erasure breeds disdain for the scholarship of Black Christians and a disdain for the engagement of a critical faith. The dismissal of Black theology is an act of racism.

This erasure robs the church of a critical understanding of its faith in addressing serious evils in our society. This erasure of Black theology is demeaning to the scholarship of Black theologians and dismissive of the voices of the modern-day prophets who speak to our stubborn, racist society. This absence not only exists in the evangelical church but in the Catholic Church as well. "It is amazing that racism could be so prevalent and violent in American life and yet so absent in white theological discourse."[21] And yet this remains the case.

LEARNING FROM BLACK THEOLOGY

Establishing a critical faith means doing one's homework and the deep work of questioning and life-long learning. However, this kind of spirituality seems rare as "most Western people are just spiritually lazy," not able to bear too much reality, and generally complacent.[22] Doing the deep work of critical faith is to question, criticize, and take risks. Richard Rohr, an American Franciscan priest and spiritual writer, contends that criticizing organized religion from within as an insider is to be faithful to the church. Giving constructive criticism from the inside, and not by throwing rocks from the outside, is the way of a critical faith.[23]

From that perspective, Rohr states that America's institutions, including the church, seldom engage the deep work of social justice, which involves embracing ambiguity, growing up spiritually, reflection critically, and living the truth. These tasks are the business of the "second half of life" according to Rohr; "second half" meaning the spiritual evolution of our faith. This meaning is not about age. Individuals who have suffered much often move to the second half of spiritual life sooner than others because they have learned from their pain.

Therefore, learning from Black theology born of pain ushers white people into counterstories of faith that expand our understanding of the scriptures and give us credibility in following Christ. For Americans, racial justice is paramount, and Black theology provides a strong biblical perspective. When this is combined with CRT, believers are better equipped to live their faith critically.

Regrettably, for some white people, embracing Black theology and CRT is a daunting task. Doing so assumes that individuals want to grow and evolve in their faith, and then it involves an admission that we might be wrong—wrong in assuming that the whole will of God begins and ends with individual conversion and salvation. Being wrong is never easy for any of us.

But slaveholders were wrong. Their interpretations of the scriptures around race were wrong. Many white Christians were wrong during Jim Crow, lynching, white flight, and segregation. Christians fiercely committed to Christ can be wrong.[24] Admitting wrongs is not impossible. In 1995, the SBC apologized for its role in slavery, Jim Crow, and lack of support of the civil rights movement. Better late than never. Given the SBC's supremacist legacy, this was big news.[25]

With humility regarding past wrongs, a commitment to reading and studying Black scholars and theologians of all denominations is a great place to begin in addressing these injustices. Black scholar activists in this genre may be small in number but are powerful in mission and purpose. Their lived experiences inform our faith and expand our understanding of what it means to be anti-racist and Christian in America.[26] They are our teachers now.

ADDING OR SUBTRACTING FROM THE GOSPEL

Conservative biblical scholars and preachers will argue that learning from Black theology is adding to or subtracting from the whole Gospel.[27] On the contrary, accepting Jesus Christ as a savior envelops both individual salvation of the soul and conversion as liberational in every sense of the word. It is liberational to the individual, to society, and to culture, with every aspect of life permeated. This is what it means to be the salt of the earth. God as embodied in the life of Christ and the power of the Holy Spirit is powerful to save individuals' souls and to liberate peoples, establish justice on earth as it is in heaven, and bring hope for eternity. No adding or subtracting here.

A working knowledge of CRT can aid in our reading of scripture and its current application. Its parallels with biblical themes are evident. CRT acknowledges the existence of evil and oppression and its permanence (Psalms 103:6; Zechariah 7:9–10); the existence of hegemonic power (Eph. 6:12); counter-storytelling, or listening to the experiences of others (Proverbs 18:13; James 1:19); the importance of examining our self-serving motives (Matthew 6:1–3); awareness of interest convergence (John 4—the Samaritan woman); the common origin of all humanity (Acts 17:26); and striving for truth and honesty in telling history (Proverbs 12:22; John 8:32). Is CRT a replacement for the Bible? Absurd. Is CRT the last word on race and racial progress? No. Is CRT as a theory helpful in understanding race in America and in the church? Absolutely!

NOTES

1 Cone, *A Black Theology of Liberation*.
2 Cone.
3 Douglass, *Narrative*.
4 Jones, *White Too Long*.
5 McCaulley, *Reading While Black*.
6 Cymbala and Blattner, *Fan the Flame*.
7 Norris, *Witnessing Whiteness*.
8 Norris.
9 Gushee, *Still Christian*.
10 Cone, *A Black Theology of Liberation*; Cone, *Black Theology & Black Power*.
11 Chisholm, personal interview.
12 Gushee, *Still Christian*.
13 McCaulley, *Reading While Black*.
14 Gutierrez, *A Theology of Liberation*.
15 McCaulley, *Reading While Black*.
16 McCaulley.
17 Brown, *Blackening of the Bible*.
18 Duncan, *Dear Church*.
19 Massingale, *Racial Justice and the Catholic Church*; Duncan, *Dear Church*.
20 McCaulley, *Reading While Black*.
21 Massingale, *Racial Justice and the Catholic Church*.
22 Cymbala and Blattner, *Fan the Flame*; Rohr, *Falling Upward*; Baldwin, *The Cross of Redemption*.
23 Rohr, *Falling Upward*.
24 Gushee, *Still Christian*.
25 Jones, *White Too Long*.
26 Massingale, *Racial Justice and the Catholic Church*.
27 Cymbala and Blattner, *Fan the Flame*.

Afterword
A Call for Critical Faith

"For the first step away from God is a distaste for learning, and lack of appetite for those things for which the soul hungers when it seeks God."

—Merton, the Desert Fathers LIII

I took a break from writing this book to watch Super Bowl LVII between the Philadelphia Phillies and the Kansas City Chiefs. With my chicken wings, onion loaf, glass of wine, and my husband and family and friends, I settled down to enjoy what has become one of America's traditions.

But don't you know, I couldn't get away from CRT. As CRT states, race permeates America because it is institutionalized, and the National Football League (NFL) is an institution. The big news was that two Black quarterbacks played for the first time in NFL history. Why should this be news? Because of the history of racism within the NFL? Then Sheryl Lee Ralph made history by singing "Lift Every Voice and Sing," the Black national anthem, live on the field. Why do we have two national anthems? And why is this historic and moving? And why did some question it as divisive? And then there was a patriotic video depicting a "history" of the United States, including several wars, but not even a glimpse of slavery, an American institution that spanned 246 years. An intentional omission and missed opportunity to tell the counterstory? Last, there was the scuttlebutt about the chief's outstanding offensive coordinator, Eric Bieniemy, who, after five years of consideration for head-coaching jobs, remains without one. Some say it is because he is Black.

Am I reading too much into the Super Bowl? Some might say: "It's just a game; lighten up!," "You can't look for race and racism in everything," "Give it up, we are moving forward," or "Eat your wings and shut up." I am not sure Colin Kaepernick would say that. And I am not sure that the many scholars who use CRT to analyze sports would agree.[1] One scholar has used CRT to query, "Can critical race theory save pro sports?" Important question.

CAN CRITICAL RACE THEORY SAVE THE CHURCH?

Only God saves the church, an institution comprised of people. CRT can help the church understand racism, engage in change, and analyze the institution. Would it not be ironic that after the opposition to Bell's theory and Bell himself, CRT is taken seriously as an analytic tool to help the church heal from its polarized and declining position as an American institution?

Unfortunately, compared to the plethora of peer review articles and scholarly publications on CRT in sports, education, law, healthcare, housing, economics, law enforcement, and criminal justice, few Christian scholars have tackled CRT and the church, unless it is to disparage the theory. I also contend that those disparaging it have not done their homework. One exception I can find to this is in Brandon Paradise's "How Critical Race Theory Marginalizes the African American Christian Tradition."[2] I disagree with some of what Paradise says, but his work is rigorous and critical. Where is the other scholarship? Where is the engagement of critical faith? The church is pulling up the rear.

As mentioned in the introduction, this was not always so. The church has a long history of the cultivation of the mind. Intellectual labor was considered essential to Martin Luther, John Calvin, Jonathan Edwards, and the Catholic intellectual tradition, exemplified by such ancients as Thomas Aquinas, Erasmus, and St. Augustine of Hippo. However, in the twentieth century, there are few Christian intellectuals other than C. S. Lewis and Reinhold Niebuhr who enjoyed the roles of Christian public intellectuals. The twentieth and twenty-first centuries' "evangelical [Christian] neglect of the mind is an aberration in a long history of Protestant efforts to give the intellect its due."[3] American revivalism placed emphasis on individualism and immediatism through the speakers' popular appeal and simple messages to mass audiences, rather than reasoned arguments appealing to the mind and the heart. Charles Finney, D. L. Moody, Billy Sunday, Billy Graham, Oral Roberts, Kenneth Copeland, Jimmy Swaggart, Jerry Falwell, John Stott, and Martyn Lloyd-Jones are in this mold.[4] This promoted a stress on personal conversion and non-traditionalism, including the abandonment of traditional learning and the life of the mind. I do not know how many times I have heard, "You do not need an education to serve the Lord." This statement is true but telling in its subtext. The underlying message is that knowledge, learning, education, and science are at best unnecessary and at worst lead to pride and evil. The life of the mind is separated from the love of God. Critical faith is not operative. And if there were ever a justice issue in America that needed the application of critical faith, it is race.

THERE IS A WOUND

If you live in America, you are wounded by racism no matter what color you happen to be. Yet, in most white churches, race and racism is treated as an issue of the past. We are instructed that we are post-racial and need to move beyond it. This avoidance does not address America's wound. Wendell Berry writes of this historical wound:

> For whatever reasons, good or bad, I have been unwilling until now to open in myself what I have known all along to be a wound—a historical wound, prepared centuries ago to come alive in me at my birth like a hereditary disease, and to be

augmented and deepened by my life. If I had thought it was only the black people who have suffered from the years of slavery and racism, then I could have dealt fully with the matter long ago; I could have filled myself with pity for them, and would no doubt have enjoyed it a great deal and thought highly of myself. But I am sure it is not so simple as that. If white people have suffered less obviously from racism than black people, they have nevertheless suffered greatly; the cost has been greater perhaps than we can yet know. . . . But the wound is there, and it is a profound disorder, as great a damage in his mind as it is in his society.[5]

Wounds not attended to and properly cleaned allow bacteria, viruses, and fungi to fester, leading in extreme cases to sepsis, organ failure, and even death. And so it is with historical wounds that are not addressed. America's history of race has not been adequately taught, discussed, or acknowledged, and damages have yet to be reconciled. The wound festers. White people and Black people live with the scars and neglect.

The irrational attack on CRT is the latest evasion of the national wound, and it is an attack led by fear. We are afraid to attend to the wound. "People in general cannot bear very much reality. . . . and the American way of life has failed—to make people happier or to make them better. Change can only happen as the truth begins to be told."[6] This truth-telling requires a critical faith, but fear is the obstacle.

Racial animus driven by fear runs deep in this country.[7] Among the white evangelical community there is an element that is among the "least spiritually healthy as they have made politics their God. There is a spiritual illness."[8] Bell describes it this way:

Unable or unwilling to perceive that there by the grace of God go I, few white people are ready to actively promote civil rights for Black people. Because of an irrational but easily roused fear that any social reform will unjustly benefit Black people, white people fail to support the programs this country desperately needs to address the widening gap between the rich and the poor, both black and white.[9]

We are complacent in calling out and addressing evil, and we are reluctant to engage in the tough questions. We avoid the wound at all costs.

CALL FOR CRITICAL FAITH

Yet who better to address the wound than the church? This is the business of the church. The scriptures tell us that there is no fear in love, that love comes from God, and that perfect love destroys fear.[10] The church is all about healing wounds and taking away fear. Is this not what Jesus is about? So where is the church? Where is the critical faith? Where is the salt of earth? Where is the love?

"There are no bystanders," and with privilege comes responsibility. The church today that separates social issues from the Gospel is guilty of the same injustices that were committed during King's day. His words apply now: "In the midst of blatant injustices inflicted upon the Negro, I have watched white churchmen stand on the sideline and mouth pious irrelevancies and sanctimonious trivialities."[11]

Churches that solely promote an individual and otherworldly gospel at the expense of embracing the Gospel that Jesus proclaimed, one of challenging evil social structures and institutions that marginalize people and oppress the poor, are increasingly impotent and aberrational as they separate the sacred and the secular, the body, and the soul. The Bible addresses Israel as a whole; God's concern is societal and His covenant was made with the people of Israel as a nation, as well as with individuals.[12]

Racism defiles the image of God and prevents bringing Christ to bear on new forms of institutionalized evil. Racism violates faith and mocks the Gospel. Critical faith equipped with good theory, like CRT, can move us toward repentance and healing. Nothing else will do.

NOTES

1 Hylton, "How to Turn"; Joseph N. Cooper, Akuoma Nwadike, and Charles Macaulay, "Big-Time Sports"; Shropshire, "Save Pro Sports?"
2 Paradise, "How Critical Race Theory."
3 Noll, *The Scandal of the Evangelical Mind.*
4 Noll.
5 Berry, *The Hidden Wound.*
6 Baldwin, *The Cross of Redemption.*
7 Duncan, *Dear Church.*
8 Massingale, *Racial Justice and the Catholic Church*; PBS, *Culture Wars.*
9 Bell, *Faces At The Bottom.*
10 Jn 4:18.
11 Luther King, *Letter from a Birmingham Jail.*
12 Rohr, *Immortal Diamond.*

Acknowledgments

Authoring this book was a lonely journey but for the support of family, friends, and colleagues. First, my husband, best friend, and personal copyeditor John R. Chaney read every word and gave sound suggestions. Just as crucial was John's ability to make me laugh and take a break from the emotional strain that the research and writing demanded. John possesses astute understanding of race in America through his lived experience and scholarly expertise, while maintaining a restrained optimism about people and the future. For your expressions of love, cups of coffee, and corny jokes through my hours of writing, I thank God.

Cathy Powell, thank you for your years of friendship. Your faith is well-grounded, your character impeccable, and your knowledge of the church deep. Upon finishing two difficult chapters, I sent them to Cathy for feedback. In part she said, "I applaud you for your undertaking. I'm not sure the subject matter will be welcomed. . . . To embrace it will mean taking action. As stated in your work, neutrality and silence puts one on the wrong side. I kind of see you going off to battle. May the Holy Spirit be your guide and wisdom, your armor and shield. May you stand firm." I cried; I was understood. What more can a writer ask for?

Then there is my dear friend Raymond Card, who after our interview and reading a chapter, wrote, "You have put to words the cry of my heart. The church should be the spearhead to vanquish racism." Ray, your encouragement through the years never waivers. You exemplify to me what it means to be a man of God.

Elliott Dawes, I appreciate your friendship and wide expertise on critical race theory. As a former student of Dr. Derrick Bell at New York University School of Law, you provided me with insights on his teaching, his character, and his faith. Elliott, I count you among my dearest colleagues.

Listening to your homily at St. Patrick's Cathedral and your wail of "Church, I just want to scream!" moved John and I to tears. It was at that moment I knew I wanted to interview you, Father Gregory Chisholm. Meeting you while authoring this book was a gift. I so enjoyed our interview and your candid responses on racism, history, and the Catholic Church. Your brilliant grasp of church history and the Bible led me to deeper research and new theologians.

Pastors Bob Smith, Seth Tidball, and Rasheed Muhammed, from different ends of America, your interviews reminded me of why I was writing. Bob, you are a kindred soul. Seth, my first pastor when I was a new Christian: You taught me the foundations of a life in Christ. Rasheed, my pastor now, thank you for those morning phone calls to pray. Three strong and loving pastors, they represent the best of the clergy.

To my colleagues at the City University of New York-LaGuardia, S. Lenise Wallace, Fern Luskin, and Emmanuel Nartey, who agreed to be interviewed and provided their valuable insights on racism in the church today (Shaunee), the underground railroad in NYC (Fern), and the Catholic Church (Emmanuel). Thanks to Andrea Francis for being my writing partner and for recognizing the emotional labor involved in this type of writing. Reem Jaafar and Shadi Haidar for all those dinners and your ongoing questions about the book—so grateful to you.

Maribel Padin-Canestro and Marla Sherman, thank you for taking the time to be interviewed and to help me see through your positionalities. Maribel, your parent advocacy is inspiring, and I now understand more about the community's response to CRT. Marla, your intelligent responses were thought-provoking and crucial to my understanding of the Evangelical Church.

Ryan Hemmer, the editor-in-chief at Fortress Press, is another gift. Meeting him in Minneapolis, it became clear that he was smart, compassionate, and understood the issues that I so passionately wanted to address. Thank you, Ryan, and the team, especially Hannah Varacalli, whose kind words and sound editing were crucial to the final product. Robert Pollock and Emily Gallagher, you bring joy to my work, and I am always pleased with your cover designs. I feel like we are kindred souls. Rachel Anderson, RMA Publicity, thank you for believing in me, and promoting my writing, and our time in Minneapolis.

Sara Jorgensen-Levy, Avril (Birdie) DeJesus, Andrea Emmanuel, Mary Zoller, Liz Barclay-Heflin, and Kurt Sealey,—my sisters and brother. Your prayers and love are felt.

Bibliography

ACLU Massachusetts. "Banned Books by Black Authors," January 31, 2022. https://www.aclum.org/en/banned-books-black-authors.

Adams, J. Christian. "Obama's Beloved Law Professor: Derrick Bell." Breitbart, March 8, 2012. https://www.breitbart.com/politics/2012/03/08/obamas-beloved-law-professor-derrick-bell/.

Addison, Meeke. "The Stated Goals of Black Lives Matter Are Anti-Christian." The Billy Graham Evangelistic Association of Canada, July 21, 2020. https://www.billygraham.ca/stories/the-stated-goals-of-black-lives-matter-are-anti-christian/.

African American Policy Forum. "A Primer on Intersectionality." Columbia Law School, n.d.

"African Americans in Minnesota | MNopedia," September 27, 2023. https://www.mnopedia.org/african-americans-minnesota.

Alberta, Tim. "How Politics Poisoned the Evangelical Church." The Atlantic, May 10, 2022. https://www.theatlantic.com/magazine/archive/2022/06/evangelical-church-pastors-political-radicalization/629631/.

Albert-Howe, Nywani. "Counterstorytelling: Intersections of Race and American Law in Derrick Bell's Science Fiction," 2013. https://DalSpace.library.dal.ca//handle/10222/36251.

———. "Counterstorytelling: Intersections of Race and American Law in Derrick Bell's Science Fiction." Dalhousie University, 2013.

Alexander, Michelle, and Cornel West. The New Jim Crow: Mass Incarceration in the Age of Colorblindness. New York: The New Press, 2012.

American Civil Liberties Union. "Mass Incarceration," September 27, 2023. https://www.aclu.org/issues/smart-justice/mass-incarceration.

American Library Association. "American Library Association Releases Preliminary Data on 2022 Book Bans." Text. News and Press Center, September 16, 2022. https://www.ala.org/news/press-releases/2022/09/ala-releases-preliminary-data-2022-book-bans.

American Museum of Natural History. "What Is a Theory? A Scientific Definition | AMNH," September 26, 2023. https://www.amnh.org/exhibitions/darwin/evolution-today/what-is-a-theory.

Annamma, Subini Ancy, Beth A. Ferri, and David J. Connor. "Disability Critical Race Theory: Exploring the Intersectional Lineage, Emergence, and Potential Futures of DisCrit in Education." *Review of Research in Education* 42, no. 1 (March 1, 2018): 46–71. https://doi.org/10.3102/0091732X18759041.

Asare, Maurice. "Debunking the Myth of Color Blindness in a Racist Society." The Bowdoin Orient, April 13, 2017. https://bowdoinorient.com/2017/04/13/debunking-the-myth-of-color-blindness-in-a-racist-society/.

Avlon, John. "Martin Luther King, Jr. a Communist? Why He's Been Whitewashed." *The Daily Beast*, January 16, 2012, sec. us-news. https://www.thedailybeast.com/articles/2012/01/16/martin-luther-king-jr-a-communist-why-he-s-been-whitewashed.

Avshalom-Smith, Devin. "Toward a Philosophy of Race: W.E.B. Du Bois and Critical Race." *1619: Journal of African Studies*, n.d.

Baker-Fletcher, Karen, trans. *Sisters of Dust, Sisters of Spirit: Womanist Wordings on God and Creation*. Minneapolis, MN: Fortress Press, 1998.

Baldwin, James. *Go Tell It on the Mountain*. Reprint edition. Vintage, 2013.

———. *The Cross of Redemption: Uncollected Writings*. Knopf Doubleday Publishing Group, 2011.

Barnum, Matt. "Did Busing for School Integration Succeed? Here's What Research Says. - Chalkbeat," September 26, 2023. https://www.chalkbeat.org/2019/7/1/21121022/did-busing-for-school-desegregation-succeed-here-s-what-research-says.

Barth, Karl. *The Doctrine of God*. Edited by G. W. Bromiley and T. F. Torrance. Translated by T. H. L. Parker and J. L. M. Haire. First English Edition. London: T&T Clark, 1957.

Bash, Dana. "Rising Hate: Antisemitism in America." Report. CNN, August 15, 2022. https://cnnpressroom.blogs.cnn.com/2022/08/15/cnn-special-report-rising-hate-antisemitism-in-america/.

Bass, S. Jonathan, James C. Cobb, and Paul Harvey. *Blessed Are the Peacemakers: Martin Luther King Jr., Eight White Religious Leaders, and the "Letter from Birmingham Jail."* Baton Rouge: LSU Press, 2001.

Baucham, Voddie. *Fault Lines: The Social Justice Movement and Evangelicalism's Looming Catastrophe*. Simon and Schuster, 2021.

———. "Looming Catastrophe," interview by Dan Andros and Tré Goins-Phillips, *Faithwire*, CNB, April 5, 2021. https://www.youtube.com/watch?v=j3LwCsRkBOE.

Bell, Derrick. *And We Are Not Saved: The Elusive Quest for Racial Justice*. San Francisco, Calif: Basic Books, 1989.

———. *Confronting Authority: Reflections of an Ardent Protester*. Boston: Beacon Pr, 1994.

———. *Ethical Ambition: Living a Life of Meaning and Worth*. Bloomsbury USA, 2003.

———. *Faces At The Bottom Of The Well: The Permanence Of Racism*. Basic Books, 1992.

———. "Brown v. Board of Education and the Interest-Convergence Dilemma." Harvard Law Review, January 11, 1980. https://harvardlawreview.org/print/no-volume/brown-v-board-of-education-and-the-interest-convergence-dilemma/.

Bernstein, Fred A. "Derrick Bell, Law Professor and Rights Advocate, Dies at 80." The New York Times, October 6, 2011, sec. U.S. https://www.nytimes.com/2011/10/06/us/derrick-bell-pioneering-harvard-law-professor-dies-at-80.html.

Berry, Wendell. The Hidden Wound. Second edition. Counterpoint, 2010.

Biden, Joseph. "Remarks by President Biden on the Continued Battle for the Soul of the Nation." The White House, September 2, 2022. https://www.whitehouse.gov/briefing-room/speeches-remarks/2022/09/01/remarks-by-president-bidenon-the-continued-battle-for-the-soul-of-the-nation/.

Blanchard, Sara, and Misasha Suzuki Graham. Dear White Women: Let's Get (Un)Comfortable Talking about Racism. The Collective Book Studio, 2021.

Blumenfeld, Warren J. "OpEd: Confronting Systemic Racism: 'Interest Convergence' at the Inflection Point." Campus Pride, July 2, 2020. https://www.campuspride.org/oped-confronting-systemic-racism-interest-convergence-at-the-inflection-point/.

Bonhoeffer, Dietrich. The Cost of Discipleship. Revised Edition. Macmillan Publishing Company, 1963.

Bonhoeffer, Dietrich, and Eric Metaxas. The Cost of Discipleship. First Edition. New York: Touchstone, 1995.

Bourlin, Olga. "Derrick Albert Bell Jr. (1930–2011).," November 15, 2013. https://www.blackpast.org/african-american-history/bell-derrick-albert-jr-1930-2011/.

Boyd, Drick, and C. T. Vivian. White Allies in the Struggle for Racial Justice. Orbis Books, 2015.

Boykin, Keith. HuffPost. "Remembering Derrick Bell," October 6, 2011. https://www.huffpost.com/entry/derrick-bell-dead_b_998024.

Breitbart. "Breitbart.Com Unveils Unedited Video of Obama and Radical Professor," n.d.

Breyer, Stephen, and Thiru Vignarajah. Breaking the Promise of Brown: The Resegregation of America's Schools. Washington: Brookings Institution Press, 2022.

Brown, Brené. Daring Greatly: How the Courage to Be Vulnerable Transforms the Way We Live, Love, Parent, and Lead. Reprint edition. New York: Avery, 2015.

Brown, David L. Critical Race Theory: A Doctrine of Devils That Is Captivating the Minds of Americans. Old Paths Publications, Incorporated, 2020.

———. Critical Race Theory: A Doctrine of Devils That Is Captivating the Minds of Americans. CRT ed. edition. Old Paths Publications, Inc, 2020.

Brown, Michael Joseph. Blackening of the Bible: The Aims of African American Biblical Scholarship. Bloomsbury Publishing USA, 2004.

———. *Blackening of the Bible: The Aims of African American Biblical Scholarship*. 1st edition. Harrisburg, Pa: Trinity Press International, 2004.

Brown, Robert McAfee. *Unexpected News: Reading the Bible with Third World Eyes*. First Edition. Westminster John Knox Press, 1984.

———. *Unexpected News: Reading the Bible with Third World Eyes*. First Edition. Philadelphia: Westminster John Knox Press, 1984.

Burnside, Tina. "African Americans in Minnesota | MNopedia," October 2, 2023. https://www.mnopedia.org/african-americans-minnesota.

Butler, Cheryl Nelson, Sherrilyn Ifill, Suzette Malveaux, Margaret E. Montoya, Natsu Taylor Saito, Nareissa L. Smith, and Tanya Washington. "The Story Behind a Letter in Support of Professor Derrick Bell." *University of Pittsburgh Law Review* 75, no. 4 (2014). https://doi.org/10.5195/lawreview.2014.353.

Butterfield, Fox. "Old Rights Campaigner Leads a Harvard Battle." *New York Times*, May 21, 1990, sec. U.S. https://www.nytimes.com/1990/05/21/us/old-rights-campaigner-leads-a-harvard-battle.html.

Carmichael, Stokely, and Charles Hamilton. *Black Power: The Politics of Liberation*. Random House, 1967.

Chalkbeat. "CRT MAP: Critical Race Theory Legislation and Schools," February 2, 2022. https://www.chalkbeat.org/22525983/map-critical-race-theory-legislation-teaching-racism.

Chan, Wing-tsit. *The Way of Lao Tzu*. New York: Pearson, 1963.

Chew, Pat. "Asian Americans: The 'Reticent' Minority and Their Paradoxes." *William & Mary Law Review* 36, no. 1 (October 1, 1994): 1.

Chisholm, Gregory, S.J. "St Charles Choir and Fr Chisholm Homily at St Patrick's Cathedral," September 27, 2023. https://venue.streamspot.com/video/136c39431c.

———. "The Cry of an Angry Black Man in a World Sick with Racism," February 12, 2021. https://www.americamagazine.org/politics-society/2021/02/12/racism-angry-black-man-homily-240005.

———. "Black History Month Homily." 2021.

Christian History Institute. "The Neglected History of Women in the Early Church | Christian History Magazine," September 27, 2023. https://christianhistoryinstitute.org/magazine/article/women-in-the-early-church.

Christopher, Tommy. "Late Prof. Derrick Bell's Widow Defends Him Against Sarah Palin and Co. 'Racist' Smear." *Mediaite* (blog), March 13, 2012. https://www.mediaite.com/tv/late-prof-derrick-bells-widow-defends-him-against-sarah-palin-and-co-racist-smear/.

"Church Sustaining," April 14, 2017. https://doi.org/10.1215/9780822372974-004.

Cobb, Jelani. "The Man Behind Critical Race Theory," September 27, 2023. https://www.newyorker.com/magazine/2021/09/20/the-man-behind-critical-race-theory.

Cobb, Jelani, and Matthew Guariglia, eds. *The Essential Kerner Commission Report*. Liveright, 2021.

Cole, Nicki Lisa. "Understanding Segregation Today." ThoughtCo, October 2, 2023. https://www.thoughtco.com/understanding-segregation-3026080.

Collins, Francis. *The Language of God: A Scientist Presents Evidence for Belief.* Simon and Schuster, 2008.

Cooper, Joseph N., and Akuoma Nwadike, and Charles Macaulay. "A Critical Race Theory Analysis of Big-Time College Sports: Implications for Culturally Responsive and Race-Conscious Sport Leadership." *Journal of Issues in Intercollegiate Athletics*, no. 10 (2017): 204–33.

Cone, James H. *Black Theology & Black Power.* Reprint edition. Maryknoll, N.Y.: Orbis Books, 1997.

——. *The Cross and the Lynching Tree.* Reprint edition. Maryknoll, NY: Orbis, 2013.

Crenshaw, Kimberlé. "Essential Reading: Demarginalizing the Intersection of Race and Sex: A Black Feminist Critique of Antidiscrimination Doctrine, Feminist Theory and Antiracist Policies." *University of Chicago Legal Forum* 1 (1989): 139–68.

——. "Op-Ed: King Was a Critical Race Theorist before There Was a Name for It - Los Angeles Times," September 26, 2023. https://www.latimes.com/opinion/story/2022-01-17/critical-race-theory-martin-luther-king.

"CRT Forward Tracking Project," September 27, 2023. https://crtforward.law.ucla.edu.

Cymbala, Jim, and John Blattner. *Fan the Flame: Let Jesus Renew Your Calling and Revive Your Church.* Grand Rapids, Michigan: Zondervan, 2022.

Davis, Angela J., ed. *Policing the Black Man: Arrest, Prosecution, and Imprisonment.* New York: Pantheon, 2017.

Dawes, Elliott (former Bell student) in discussion with the author, November 21, 2022.

Delgado, Richard. "Storytelling for Oppositionists and Others: A Plea for Narrative." SSRN Scholarly Paper. Rochester, NY, August 1, 1989. https://papers.ssrn.com/abstract=1577362.

Delgado, Richard, and Jean Stefancic. *Critical Race Theory: An Introduction.* NYU Press, 2012.

Delmont, Matthew F. *Half American: The Epic Story of African Americans Fighting World War II at Home and Abroad.* Viking, 2022.

Denison Forum. "Is Critical Race Theory Marxist?," September 26, 2023. https://www.denisonforum.org/resources/is-critical-race-theory-marxist/.

DeSalle, Rob, and Ian Tattersall. *Troublesome Science: The Misuse of Genetics and Genomics in Understanding Race.* Columbia University Press, 2018.

"DeSantis: Critical Race Theory Teaches 'Kids To Hate This Country'; Pushes Legislative Proposal To Strengthen Enforcement Against It - CBS Miami," January 10, 2022. https://www.cbsnews.com/miami/news/desantis-critical-race-theory-florida-legislative-session/.

DiAngelo, Robin, and Michael Eric Dyson. *White Fragility: Why It's So Hard for White People to Talk About Racism.* Reprint edition. Boston: Beacon Press, 2018.

Dodson, Dr. Mary L. *Critical Race Theory Versus God's Divine Law: Making a Choice*. Watchman Call Press, 2021.

Douglass, Frederick. *Narrative of the Life of Frederick Douglass: An American Slave, Written by Himself.* Edited by David W. Blight. 2nd edition. Boston: Bedford/St. Martin's, 2002.

Du Bois, W. E. B, and David Levering Lewis. *Black Reconstruction in America, 1860-1880*. 12.2.1997 edition. New York: Free Press, 1998.

Duncan, Lenny. *Dear Church: A Love Letter from a Black Preacher to the Whitest Denomination in the US*. Fortress Press, 2019.

Dyson, Michael Eric. *Tears We Cannot Stop: A Sermon to White America*. 1st edition. St. Martin's Press, 2017.

Edmiston, Kelly. "Theological Gaslighting as Spiritual Abuse." Jesus Creed | A Blog by Scot McKnight, September 27, 2023. https://www.christianitytoday.com/scot-mcknight/2020/december/theological-gaslighting-as-spiritual-abuse.html.

Edwards, Korie Little. *The Elusive Dream: The Power of Race in Interracial Churches*. Illustrated edition. New York: Oxford University Press, 2008.

———. "The Multiethnic Church Movement Hasn't Lived up to Its Promise." ChristianityToday.com, February 16, 2021. https://www.christianitytoday.com/ct/2021/march/race-diversity-multiethnic-church-movement-promise.html.

Ekman, Mattias. "The Great Replacement: Strategic Mainstreaming of Far-Right Conspiracy Claims." *Convergence* 28, no. 4 (August 1, 2022): 1127–43. https://doi.org/10.1177/13548565221091983.

ELCA. "ELCA Anti-Racism Pledge," September 27, 2023. https://www.elca.org:443/racialjusticepledge.

Eligon, John, and Tim Arango. "Ten Months After George Floyd's Death, Minneapolis Residents Are at War Over Policing." *New York Times*, March 28, 2021, sec. U.S. https://www.nytimes.com/2021/03/28/us/minneapolis-george-floyd.html.

Ellis, Justin. "Minneapolis Had This Coming." *The Atlantic* (blog), June 9, 2020. https://www.theatlantic.com/ideas/archive/2020/06/minneapolis-long-overdue-crisis/612826/.

Emerson, Michael O. "Mosaix Global Newsletter.," December 2019.

Emerson, Michael O., and Christian Smith. *Divided by Faith: Evangelical Religion and the Problem of Race in America*. 34320th edition. Oxford: Oxford University Press, 2001.

Evans, Rachel Held, and Sarah Bessey. *Faith Unraveled: How a Girl Who Knew All the Answers Learned to Ask Questions*. Zondervan, 2014.

Fairbanks, Daniel J. *Everyone Is African: How Science Explodes the Myth of Race*. Illustrated edition. Amherst, NY: Prometheus, 2015.

First Witness Child Advocacy Center. "White Privilege: Unpacking the Invisible Knapsack," September 27, 2023. https://firstwitness.org/resources/white-privilege-unpacking-the-invisible-knapsack/.

Fischl, Richard Michael. "'Some Realism About Critical Legal Studies' by Richard Michael Fischl," September 26, 2023. https://repository.law.miami.edu/umlr/vol41/iss3/4/.

Fort, Nyle. "The Religion of Protest." The Cut, January 31, 2022. https://www.thecut.com/2022/01/black-lives-matter-religion-spirituality.html.

Fox, Jeff. "10 Fallacies Of Using 'All Lives Matter' As A Response." *Medium* (blog), June 14, 2020. https://jefffox-84712.medium.com/10-fallacies-of-using-all-lives-matter-as-a-response-7cb8071958d4.

Fox News. "Hannity." Collection. Fox News, September 26, 2023. https://www.foxnews.com/shows/hannity.

Fox News. "The Words of Derrick Bell." Fox News, March 24, 2015. https://www.foxnews.com/transcript/the-words-of-derrick-bell.

Freire, Paulo, and Donaldo Macedo. *Pedagogy of the Oppressed, 30th Anniversary Edition*. Translated by Myra Bergman Ramos. 30th Anniversary edition. New York: Continuum, 2000.

Gates, Henry Louis, Jr. *"Culture Wars in Black & White"* The 2022 Hutchins Forum, PBS, August 17, 2022. https://www.youtube.com/watch?v=ChaQAF5Vwg8.

George, Janel. "A Lesson on Critical Race Theory," September 26, 2023. https://www.americanbar.org/groups/crsj/publications/human_rights_magazine_home/civil-rights-reimagining-policing/a-lesson-on-critical-race-theory/.

Gillborn, David. "Intersectionality, Critical Race Theory, and the Primacy of Racism: Race, Class, Gender, and Disability in Education." *Qualitative Inquiry* 21, no. 3 (March 1, 2015): 277–87. https://doi.org/10.1177/1077800414557827.

Glaude, Eddie S., Jr. *Begin Again: James Baldwin's America and Its Urgent Lessons for Our Own*. New York: Crown, 2020.

———. *Democracy in Black: How Race Still Enslaves the American Soul*. Reprint edition. Crown, 2016.

Gonzalez, Mike. "Purging Whiteness To Purge Capitalism." The Heritage Foundation, September 26, 2023. https://www.heritage.org/progressivism/commentary/purging-whiteness-purge-capitalism.

Gordon, Lewis R. "'A Short History of the Critical in Critical Race Theory.'" *Newsletter on Philosophy, Law, and the Black Experience* 98, no. 2 (Spring 1999).

Gottlieb, Alma. "Why 'The Great Replacement Theory' Is Not a Theory, and Why That Matters," May 18, 2022. https://almagottlieb.com/2022/05/17/why-the-great-replacement-theory-is-not-a-theory-and-why-that-matters/.

Griswold, Kaila. "Author and Activist Tim Wise Defends Critical Race Theory - The Johns Hopkins News-Letter," September 26, 2023. https://www.jhunewsletter.com/article/2021/11/author-and-activist-tim-wise-defends-critical-race-theory.

Gushee, David P. *Still Christian: Following Jesus Out of American Evangelicalism*. 2nd edition. Westminster John Knox Press, 2017.

Gushee, David P., Phyllis Tickle, and Brian D. McLaren. *Changing Our Mind, Second Edition*. 2nd edition. Read the Spirit Books, 2015.

Gutierrez, Gustavo. *A Theology of Liberation: History, Politics, and Salvation.* Revised edition. Maryknoll, NY: Orbis Books, 1988.

Hadden Loh, Tracy, Christopher Coes, and Becca Buthe. "Separate and Unequal: Persistent Residential Segregation Is Sustaining Racial and Economic Injustice in the U.S." Brookings, October 2, 2023. https://www.brookings.edu/articles/trend-1-separate-and-unequal-neighborhoods-are-sustaining-racial-and-economic-injustice-in-the-us/.

Hannity, Sean. Breitbart.com Unveils Unedited Video of Obama and Radical Professor, March 7, 2012. http://www.foxnews.com/on-air/hannity/2012/03/08/exclusivebreitbartcom-unveils-unedited-video-obama-and-radical-professor.

———. I Don't Know How Obama Can Sleep at Night with Maher's 'Dirty Money', March 9, 2012. http://www.foxnews.com/on-air/hannity/2012/03/09/palin-i-dontknow-how-obama-can-sleep-night-mahers-dirty-money.

Harper, Lisa Sharon. "An Open Letter to Franklin Graham." Sojourners, March 19, 2015. https://sojo.net/articles/open-letter-franklin-graham.

———. "An Open Letter to Franklin Graham." Sojourners, March 19, 2015. https://sojo.net/articles/open-letter-franklin-graham.

Harris, Cheryl I. "Whiteness as Property." *Harvard Law Review* 106, no. 8 (1993): 1707–91. https://doi.org/10.2307/1341787.

———. "Whiteness as Property." Harvard Law Review, June 10, 1993. https://harvardlawreview.org/print/no-volume/whiteness-as-property/.

Health Affairs. "Health, Income, & Poverty: Where We Are & What Could Help," September 27, 2023. https://www.healthaffairs.org/do/10.1377/hpb20180817.901935/full/.

Herzog, William R., II. *Parables as Subversive Speech: Jesus as Pedagogue of the Oppressed.* 1st edition. Westminster John Knox Press, 1994.

Hill, Daniel, and Brenda Salter McNeil. *White Awake: An Honest Look at What It Means to Be White.* IVP, 2017.

Hoby, Hermione. "Toni Morrison: 'I'm Writing for Black People . . . I Don't Have to Apologise.'" *The Guardian*, April 25, 2015, sec. Books. https://www.theguardian.com/books/2015/apr/25/toni-morrison-books-interview-god-help-the-child.

Holmes, D.L. "The Founding Fathers, Deism, and Christianity." In *Encyclopedia Britannica*, December 21, 2006.

Hooten, Kyle. "Minneapolis To Install Permanent Monument To George Floyd." Alpha News, July 21, 2020. https://alphanews.org/floyd-monument/.

Hudson, Winson, and Constance Curry. *Mississippi Harmony: Memoirs of a Freedom Fighter.* New York: Palgrave Macmillan, 2002.

"Human Geneticists Curb Use of the Term 'Race' in Their Papers," September 27, 2023. https://www.science.org/content/article/human-geneticists-curb-use-term-race-their-papers.

Hylton, Kevin. "How a Turn to Critical Race Theory Can Contribute to Our Understanding of 'Race', Racism and Anti-Racism in Sport." *International*

Review for the Sociology of Sport 45, no. 3 (September 1, 2010): 335–54. https://doi.org/10.1177/1012690210371045.

"I Just Want to Do God's Will . . . ," CBN, September 26, 2023. https://www.cbn.com/special/blackhistory/ats_mlk_salvation.aspx.

Isichei, Elizabeth. *A History of Christianity in Africa: From Antiquity to the Present*. Eerdmans, 1995.

Johnson, Hannibal B. *Black Wall Street 100: An American City Grapples With Its Historical Racial Trauma*. Illustrated edition. Eakin Press, 2020.

Jones, Robert P. *The End of White Christian America*. Reprint edition. Simon & Schuster, 2016.

———. *White Too Long: The Legacy of White Supremacy in American Christianity*. Illustrated edition. New York: Simon & Schuster, 2020.

Jones, Roudabeh Kishi, Melissa Pavlik, Elliott Bynum, Adam Miller, Curtis Goos, Josh Satre, Sam. "ACLED 2020: The Year in Review." *ACLED* (blog), March 18, 2021. https://acleddata.com/2021/03/18/acled-2020-the-year-in-review/.

Kahn-Cullors, Patrisse. *When They Call You a Terrorist: A Black Lives Matter Memoir*. 1st edition. St. Martin's Press, 2018.

Kendi, Ibram X. *How to Be an Antiracist*. First Edition. New York: One World, 2019.

———. *Stamped from the Beginning: The Definitive History of Racist Ideas in America*. Reprint edition. New York: Bold Type Books, 2017.

———. "There Is No Debate Over Critical Race Theory." *The Atlantic* (blog), July 9, 2021. https://www.theatlantic.com/ideas/archive/2021/07/opponents-critical-race-theory-are-arguing-themselves/619391/.

Kennedy, John W. "Racism Resolution Revisited." PENews, June 26, 2020. https://news.ag.org/en/news/racism-resolution-revisited.

Kennedy, Lesley. "Voting Rights Milestones in America: A Timeline." HISTORY, August 15, 2023. https://www.history.com/news/voting-rights-timeline.

King, Martin Luther, Jr. *Letter from a Birmingham Jail*. Penguin UK, 2018.

Kristof, Nicholas. "Opinion | Pull Yourself Up by Bootstraps? Go Ahead, Try It." *New York Times*, February 20, 2020, sec. Opinion. https://www.nytimes.com/2020/02/19/opinion/economic-mobility.html.

Kroeger, Catherine. "The Neglected History of Women in the Early Church." *Christian History*, 1988. https://christianhistoryinstitute.org/magazine/issue/women-in-the-early-church/.

Labbé-DeBose, Theola. "Black Women Are among Country's Most Religious Groups." *Washington Post*, July 6, 2012. https://www.washingtonpost.com/local/black-women-are-among-countrys-most-religious-groups/2012/07/06/gJQA0BksSW_story.html.

Lackey, Darrell and Divergence. "CRT In Light of Ephesians 6:12." *Divergence* (blog), June 26, 2021. https://www.patheos.com/blogs/divergence/2021/06/26/crt-in-light-of-ephesians-612/.

———. "CRT In Light of Ephesians 6:12." *Divergence* (blog), June 26, 2021. https://www.patheos.com/blogs/divergence/2021/06/26/crt-in-light-of-ephesians-612/.

Lee, Barbara. "Congresswoman Barbara Lee: Resisting The Rise Of Hatred In The Era Of Trump | Barbara Lee - Congresswoman for the 12th District of California," June 13, 2017. https://lee.house.gov/news/articles/congress-woman-barbara-lee-resisting-the-rise-of-hatred-in-the-era-of-trump_.

Lee, Morgan. "Critical Race Theory: What Christians Need to Know." ChristianityToday.com, July 2, 2021. https://www.christianitytoday.com/ct/podcasts/quick-to-listen/critical-race-theory-racism-evangelicals-divided-podcast.html.

Legg, Mark. "Is Critical Race Theory Marxist?" Denison Forum, October 2, 2023. https://www.denisonforum.org/resources/is-critical-race-theory-marxist/.

Lesperance, Diana. *Critical Race Theory: An Introduction from a Biblical and Historical Perspective.* Independently published, 2020.

Levin, Sam. "Black Lives Matter Grassroots Chapters Sue Global Foundation over Funds." *The Guardian*, September 2, 2022, sec. World news. https://www.theguardian.com/world/2022/sep/02/black-lives-matter-grassroots-lawsuit-global-foundation.

Lleras, Christy. "Race, Racial Concentration, and the Dynamics of Educational Inequality Across Urban and Suburban Schools." *American Educational Research Journal* 45, no. 4 (2008): 886–912.

Lorde, Geraldine Audre. *Sister Outsider: Essays and Speeches.* Trumansburg, NY: Crossing Press, 1984.

Lovelace, Vanessa. "Womanist Biblical Interpretation." *Bible Odyssey* (blog), 2023. https://www.bibleodyssey.org/passages/related-articles/womanist-biblical-interpretation/.

Lucas, Lawrence E. *Black Priest White Church: Catholics and Racism.* Trenton, NJ: Africa World Pr, 1989.

——. *Black Priest/White Church;: Catholics and Racism.* First Edition. Random House, 1970.

Luo, Michael. "The Wasting of the Evangelical Mind." *New Yorker*, March 4, 2021. https://www.newyorker.com/news/daily-comment/the-wasting-of-the-evangelical-mind.

Malcolm, Kari Torjesen. *Women at the Crossroads: A Path Beyond Feminism and Traditionalism.* Trade Paperback edition. Downers Grove, Ill: Intervarsity Pr, 1982.

Mandelaro, Jim. "Ibram X. Kendi: 'The Very Heartbeat of Racism Is Denial.'" *News Center* (blog), February 25, 2021. https://www.rochester.edu/newscenter/ibram-x-kendi-the-very-heartbeat-of-racism-is-denial-470332/.

Massingale, Bryan N. "Black Faith Matters: Harlem." Sheen Center for Thought and Culture, New York, February 4, 2023.

——. *Racial Justice and the Catholic Church.* 3/22/10 edition. Maryknoll, N.Y: Orbis Books, 2010.

MasterClass. "Derrick Bell: Critical Race Theory Scholar and Law Professor - 2023," September 26, 2023. https://www.masterclass.com/articles/derrick-bell-guide.

Matsuda, Mari. "Looking to the Bottom: Critical Legal Studies and Reparations," 1987. http://hdl.handle.net/10125/65944.

Mayo Clinic. "Why Are People of Color More at Risk of Being Affected by COVID-19?," September 27, 2023. https://www.mayoclinic.org/diseases-conditions/coronavirus/expert-answers/coronavirus-infection-by-race/faq-20488802.

Mccann-Mortimer, Patricia, Martha Augoustinos, and Amanda Lecouteur. "'Race' and the Human Genome Project: Constructions of Scientific Legitimacy." *Discourse & Society* 15, no. 4 (July 1, 2004): 409–32. https://doi.org/10.1177/0957926504043707.

McCaulley, Esau. *Reading While Black: African American Biblical Interpretation as an Exercise in Hope.* IVP Academic, 2020.

McIntosh, Peggy. "White Privilege: Unpacking the Invisible Knapsack," 1989. https://issuu.com/maoriachievementcollaborative/docs/white_privilege-_unpacking_the_invisible_knapsack_.

Mediaite. "Late Prof. Derrick Bell's Widow Defends Him Against Sarah Palin And Co. 'Racist' Smear," March 13, 2012. https://www.mediaite.com/tv/late-prof-derrick-bells-widow-defends-him-against-sarah-palin-and-co-racist-smear/.

Merton, Thomas. *The Wisdom of the Desert.* Revised edition. New Directions, 1970.

———. *The Wisdom of the Desert: Sayings from the Desert Fathers of the Fourth Century.* A New Directions, 1960.

Mills, C. Wright. *The Sociological Imagination.* 40th Anniversary Edition. New York: Oxford University Press, 2000.

Morrison, Aaron. "AP Exclusive: Black Lives Matter Opens up about Its Finances." AP News, February 23, 2021. https://apnews.com/article/black-lives-matter-90-million-finances-8a80cad199f54c0c4b9e74283d27366f.

Morrison, D. "Whose Interests and Under Whose Control? Interest Convergence in Science-Focused School-Community Collaborations." *Cultural Studies in Education* 13, no. 1 (2018): 86–91.

Mulder, Mark T. "Evangelical Church Polity and the Nuances of White Flight: A Case Study from the Roseland and Englewood Neighborhoods in Chicago." *Journal of Urban History* 38, no. 1 (2012): 16–38. https://doi.org/10.1177/0096144211420637.

Myers, Samuel L., and Inhyuck Ha. *Race Neutrality: Rationalizing Remedies to Racial Inequality.* Rowman & Littlefield, 2018.

Mz manynames. "Attributing Words." *U.S. Against Equine Slaughter* (blog), November 3, 2008. http://unnecessaryevils.blogspot.com/2008/11/attributing-words.html.

Nadeem, Reem. "Modeling the Future of Religion in America." *Pew Research Center's Religion & Public Life Project* (blog), September 13, 2022. https://www.pewresearch.org/religion/2022/09/13/modeling-the-future-of-religion-in-america/.

National Catholic Reporter. "The Assumptions of White Privilege and What We Can Do about It," September 27, 2023. https://www.ncronline.org/opinion/guest-voices/assumptions-white-privilege-and-what-we-can-do-about-it.

National Council of Churches. "Faith and Facts for H.R. 40 - Commission to Study and Develop Reparation Proposals for African Americans Act," n.d. http://nationalcouncilofchurches.us/wp-content/uploads/2021/04/NCC-HR-40-Faith-and-Facts-FINAL.pdf.

———. "Reparatory Justice," September 29, 2023. https://nationalcouncilof churches.us/a-c-t-now-to-end-racism/reparations/.

National Geographic. "There's No Scientific Basis for Race—It's a Made-up Label," March 12, 2018. https://www.nationalgeographic.com/magazine/article/race-genetics-science-africa.

National History Museum. "The Way We Have Been Thinking about the First Modern Humans in Africa Could Be Wrong," September 27, 2023. https://www.nhm.ac.uk/discover/news/2018/july/the-way-we-think-about-the-first-modern-humans-in-africa.html.

National Human Genome Research Institute. "15 Ways Genomics Influences Our World," December 2019. https://www.genome.gov/dna-day/15-ways.

NBC News. "The Ed Show for Monday, March 12, 2012," March 13, 2012. https://www.nbcnews.com/id/wbna46720403.

Newman, Joe. *Race and the Assemblies of God Church: The Journey from Azusa Street to the Miracle of Memphis.* Youngstown, N.Y: Cambria Press, 2007.

Nodjimbadem, Katie. "Sojourner Truth and the Unfinished Fight for Equality." *New Yorker,* August 14, 2020. https://www.newyorker.com/culture/video-dept/sojourner-truth-and-the-unfinished-fight-for-equality.

Noll, Mark A. *The Scandal of the Evangelical Mind.* Grand Rapids, MI: Eerdmans, 1995.

———. *The Scandal of the Evangelical Mind.* Grand Rapids, MI: Eerdmans, 1995.

Norris, Kristopher. *Witnessing Whiteness: Confronting White Supremacy in the American Church.* New York: Oxford University Press, 2020.

Nortey, Justin. "Most White Americans Who Regularly Attend Worship Services Voted for Trump in 2020." *Pew Research Center* (blog), September 27, 2023. https://www.pewresearch.org/short-reads/2021/08/30/most-white-americans-who-regularly-attend-worship-services-voted-for-trump-in-2020/.

Omi, Michael, and Howard Winant. *Racial Formation in the United States: From the 1960s to the 1990s.* 2nd ed. New York London: Routledge, 1994.

Packer, ZZ. "What Happens to a Professor When His Theory of Anti-Racism Goes Mainstream?" GQ, August 20, 2020. https://www.gq.com/story/ibram-x-kendi-antiracism-scholar-profile.

Painter, Nell Irvin. *Sojourner Truth: A Life, A Symbol.* Revised ed. edition. New York: W. W. Norton & Company, 1997.

Pape, Robert A. "Deep, Divisive, Disturbing, and Continuing" October 2, 2023. https://cpost.uchicago.edu/publications/deep_divisive_disturbing_and_continuing_new_survey_shows_maintream_support_for_violence_to_restore_trump_remains_strong/.

Paradise, Brandon. "How Critical Race Theory Marginalizes the African American Christian Tradition." *Michigan Journal of Race and Law* 20, no. 1 (October 1, 2014): 117–211.

Pascal, Blaise. *Pensées and Other Writings.* Edited by Anthony Levi. Translated by Honor Levi. New York: Oxford University Press, 2008.

Pavid, Katie. "The Way We Have Been Thinking about the First Modern Humans in Africa Could Be Wrong." Natural History Museum, July 11, 2018. https://www.nhm.ac.uk/discover/news/2018/july/the-way-we-think-about-the-first-modern-humans-in-africa.html.

PEN America. "Banned in the USA: Rising School Book Bans Threaten Free Expression and Students' First Amendment Rights (April 2022)," April 7, 2022. https://pen.org/banned-in-the-usa/.

PENews. "Racism Resolution Revisited," June 26, 2020. https://news.ag.org/en/news/racism-resolution-revisited.

Pérez Ortega, Rodrigo. "Human Geneticists Curb Use of the Term 'Race' in Their Papers," September 28, 2023. https://www.science.org/content/article/human-geneticists-curb-use-term-race-their-papers.

Piaget, Jean, and Barbel Inhelder. *The Psychology of The Child.* 2nd edition. New York: Basic Books, 1969.

Public School Review. "Minnetonka Senior High School (2023-24 Ranking) - Minnetonka, MN," September 20, 2023. https://www.publicschoolreview.com/minnetonka-senior-high-school-profile.

Quinn, Karl. "Are All White People Racist? Why Critical Race Theory Has Us Rattled." *Sydney Morning Herald*, November 6, 2020. https://www.smh.com.au/culture/books/are-all-white-people-racist-why-critical-race-theory-has-us-rattled-20201105-p56bwv.html.

"RACE - The Power of an Illusion. About the Series | PBS," September 27, 2023. https://www.pbs.org/race/000_About/002_04-about-01-01.htm.

Radice, Joy. "Derrick Bell's Community-Based Classroom." *Columbia Journal of Race and Law* Special Feature (January 1, 2012): 44–48.

Rah, Soong-Chan, and Brenda Salter McNeil. *Prophetic Lament: A Call for Justice in Troubled Times.* Downers Grove: IVP, 2015.

———. *Prophetic Lament: A Call for Justice in Troubled Times.* IVP, 2015.

"Rev. Dr. Paul Smith | Derrick Bell," September 26, 2023. https://professorderrickbell.com/tributes/rev-paul-smith/.

Rodrigues, Michelle A., Ruby Mendenhall, and Kathryn B.H. Clancy. "'There's Realizing, and Then There's Realizing': How Social Support Can Counter Gaslighting of Women of Color Scientists." *Journal of Women and Minorities in Science and Engineering* 27, no. 2 (2021): 1–23. https://doi.org/10.1615/JWomenMinorScienEng.2020034630.

Rohr, Richard. *Falling Upward: A Spirituality for the Two Halves of Life -- A Companion Journal.* 1st edition. Jossey-Bass, 2013.

———. *Immortal Diamond: The Search for Our True Self.* 1st edition. Jossey-Bass, 2013.

———. "Lots of Priests, Not So Many Prophets." Homilies, CAC Podcasts, 2023. https://www.youtube.com/watch?v=00ciG6sRQXA.

Salter, Jim. "A Puzzling Number of Men Tied to the Ferguson Protests Have since Died." *Chicago Tribune,* March 18, 2019. https://www.chicagotribune.com/nation-world/ct-ferguson-activist-deaths-black-lives-matter-20190317-story.html.

Sanneh, Kelefa. "The Fight to Redefine Racism." *New Yorker,* August 12, 2019. https://www.newyorker.com/magazine/2019/08/19/the-fight-to-redefine-racism.

Schultz, Ed. "The Ed Show," NBC, March 12, 2012. https://www.nbcnews.com/id/wbna46720403.

Schwartz, Joni, and John R. Chaney. *Gifts from the Dark: Learning from the Incarceration Experience.* Lanham Boulder New York London: Lexington Books, 2021.

Schwartz, Joni, and Rebecca Schwartz. *Learning to Disclose.* New York: Peter Lang, 2020.

Segura, Olga M. *Birth of a Movement: Black Lives Matter and the Catholic Church.* Maryknoll, NY: Orbis, 2021.

Seligman, Amanda I. *Block by Block: Neighborhoods and Public Policy on Chicago's West Side.* 1st edition. Chicago, IL: University of Chicago Press, 2005.

Sharp, Joshua. "Voices: The Supernatural Battle against Systemic Racism." *Baptist Standard,* June 10, 2020. https://www.baptiststandard.com/opinion/voices/the-supernatural-battle-against-systemic-racism/.

Shropshire, Kenneth L. "Can Critical Race Theory Save pro Sports?" The Philadelphia Citizen, October 20, 2021. https://thephiladelphiacitizen.org/can-critical-race-theory-save-pro-sports/.

Smithsonian Folkways Recordings. "Lead Belly: The Smithsonian Folkways Collection," September 27, 2023. https://folkways.si.edu/leadbelly.

Southern Baptist Church. "On Critical Race Theory and Intersectionality - SBC.Net." https://www.sbc.net/, June 1, 2019. https://www.sbc.net/resource-library/resolutions/on-critical-race-theory-and-intersectionality/.

———. "Resolution On Racial Reconciliation on the 150th Anniversary of the Southern Baptist Convention," September 27, 2023. https://www.sbc.net/resource-library/resolutions/resolution-on-racial-reconciliation-on-the-150th-anniversary-of-the-southern-baptist-convention/.

Sparks, Dana. "Coronavirus Infection by Race: What's behind the Health Disparities?" Mayo Clinic News Network, August 7, 2020. https://newsnetwork.mayoclinic.org/discussion/coronavirus-infection-by-race-whats-behind-the-health-disparities/.

Spock, Benjamin. *Decent and Indecent: Our Personal and Political Behavior.* New York: McCall, 1970.

Stauffer, Cole. "When Polarization Hits the Pews." Vanderbilt University, September 26, 2023. https://www.vanderbilt.edu/unity/2021/02/22/when-polarization-hits-the-pews/.

Strachan, Owen, and John MacArthur. *Christianity and Wokeness: How the Social Justice Movement Is Hijacking the Gospel—and the Way to Stop It.* Salem Books, 2021.

Stout, Catherine, and Thomas Wilburn. "CRT MAP: Critical Race Theory Legislation and Schools." Chalkbeat, February 2, 2022. https://www.chalkbeat.org/22525983/map-critical-race-theory-legislation-teaching-racism.

Suran, Melissa. "The Separation of Church and Science." *EMBO Reports* 11, no. 8 (2010): 586–89. https://doi.org/10.1038/embor.2010.106.

———. "The Separation of Church and Science." *EMBO Reports* 11, no. 8 (August 2010): 586–89. https://doi.org/10.1038/embor.2010.106.

Swain, Carol. *Pat Robertson and Dr. Swain Discuss Critical Race Theory on the 700 Club - Extended Version*, 2021. https://www.youtube.com/watch?v=uAw3Eva_F6s.

Swarns, Rachel L. "Catholic Order Pledges $100 Million to Atone for Slave Labor and Sales." *New York Times*, March 15, 2021, sec. U.S. https://www.nytimes.com/2021/03/15/us/jesuits-georgetown-reparations-slavery.html.

Talbot, Louis T. *Bible Questions Explained.* 1st edition. CreateSpace Independent Publishing Platform, 2014.

Talesnik, Dana. "Kendi Expounds on Defeating Racism." NIH Record, November 11, 2022. https://nihrecord.nih.gov/2022/11/11/kendi-expounds-defeating-racism.

Taylor, George. "Race, Religion, and Law: The Tension Between Spirit and Its Institutionalization." *University of Maryland Law Journal of Race, Religion, Gender and Class* 6, no. 1 (January 1, 2006): 51.

———. "Racism as 'The Nation's Crucial Sin': Theology and Derrick Bell." *Michigan Journal of Race and Law* 9, no. 2 (January 1, 2004): 269–322.

Terrell, Mary Church. "What Role Is the Educated Negro Woman to Play in The Uplifting of Her Race?" In *Twentieth Century Negro Literature*, 1902.

The Armed Conflict Location and Event Data Project. "2020 Annual Report," 2020

———. "2021 Annual Report," 2021

The Episcopal Church. "Racial Justice Audit," October 2, 2023. https://www.episcopalchurch.org/ministries/racial-reconciliation/racial-justice-audit/.

"The Founding Fathers, Deism, and Christianity | Christianity, Enlightenment & Religion | Britannica," September 27, 2023. https://www.britannica.com/topic/The-Founding-Fathers-Deism-and-Christianity-1272214.

"'The Great Replacement:' An Explainer | ADL," September 26, 2023. https://www.adl.org/resources/backgrounder/great-replacement-explainer.

The New York Times. "The 1619 Project." August 14, 2019, sec. Magazine. https://www.nytimes.com/interactive/2019/08/14/magazine/1619-america-slavery.html.

"This Far by Faith. Sojourner Truth | PBS," October 2, 2023. https://www.pbs. org/thisfarbyfaith/people/sojourner_truth.html.

ThoughtCo. "Understanding Segregation Today," September 27, 2023. https:// www.thoughtco.com/understanding-segregation-3026080.

Thurman, Howard, and Vincent Harding. *Jesus and the Disinherited*. Reprint edition. Boston, MA: Beacon Press, 1996.

Tisby, Jemar, and Lecrae Moore. *The Color of Compromise: The Truth about the American Church's Complicity in Racism*. Zondervan, 2019.

———. *The Color of Compromise: The Truth about the American Church's Complicity in Racism*. Grand Rapids, Michigan: Zondervan, 2020.

Touré. "No, Newsmax, Interracial Marriage Doesn't Prove Systemic Racism Isn't Real." TheGrio, April 28, 2022. https://thegrio.com/2022/04/28/ no-newsmax-interracial-marriage-doesnt-mean-system-racism-isnt-real/.

Tranby, Eric, and Douglas Hartmann. "Critical Whiteness Theories and the Evangelical 'Race Problem': Extending Emerson and Smith's 'Divided by Faith.'" *Journal for the Scientific Study of Religion* 47, no. 3 (2008): 341–359.

USCCB. "Brothers and Sisters to Us | USCCB," September 27, 2023. https://www. usccb.org/committees/african-american-affairs/brothers-and-sisters-us.

Vicari, Chelsen. "7 Sojourner Truth Quotes on Equality Grounded in Faith." Juicy Ecumenism, February 13, 2017. https://juicyecumenism. com/2017/02/13/7-sojourner-truth-quotes-equality-grounded-faith/.

Walker, Alice. *In Search of Our Mothers' Gardens: Womanist Prose*. San Diego: Harcourt, Brace & Jovanovich, 1983.

Walker, Malea. "Sojourner Truth's Most Famous Speech | Headlines and Heroes." Webpage. The Library of Congress, April 7, 2021. //blogs.loc. gov/headlinesandheroes/2021/04/sojourner-truths-most-famous-speech.

Walker, V. "Critical Race Theory: The New White Supremacy." *Freedom Center* (blog), April 6, 2021.

Wallis, Jim, and Bryan Stevenson. *America's Original Sin: Racism, White Privilege, and the Bridge to a New America*. First Edition. Grand Rapids: Brazos Press, 2016.

———. *America's Original Sin: Racism, White Privilege, and the Bridge to a New America*. Reprint edition. Brazos Press, 2017.

WATCH LIVE: "Culture Wars in Black & White" - The 2022 Hutchins Forum, 2022. https://www.youtube.com/watch?v=ChaQAF5Vwg8.

Watson, Richard. *Cogito, Ergo Sum: The Life of Rene Descartes*. Revised edition. Boston: David R. Godine, Publisher, 2007.

Weeks, Lee. "Critical Race Theory: A Dangerous Ideology." The Billy Graham Evangelistic Association of Canada, October 21, 2021. https://www. billygraham.ca/stories/critical-race-theory-a-dangerous-ideology/.

West, Gerald O. *Biblical Hermeneutics of Liberation: Modes of Reading the Bible in the South African Context*. Revised edition. Maryknoll, NY: Orbis Books, 1995.

Whitmire, Kyle. "Lawmaker Wants to Ban CRT, I Asked Him What It Is." al, June 15, 2021. https://www.al.com/news/2021/06/whitmire-alabama-lawmaker-wants-to-ban-critical-race-theory-so-i-asked-him-what-it-is.html.

Wilkerson, Isabel. *Caste: The Origins of Our Discontents*. Reprint edition. New York: Random House, 2020.

Williams, Reggie L. *Bonhoeffer's Black Jesus: Harlem Renaissance Theology and an Ethic of Resistance*. Waco, Texas: Baylor University Press, 2014.

Wink, Walter. *Naming the Powers: The Language of Power in the New Testament*. Illustrated edition. Philadelphia: Fortress Press, 1984.

Winstead, Brandon. "'Evangelize the Negro': Segregation, Power, and Evangelization within the Church of the Nazarene's Gulf Central District, 1953–1969," November 21, 2022.

Yoo, William. *What Kind of Christianity: A History of Slavery and Anti-Black Racism in the Presbyterian Church*. Westminster John Knox Press, 2022.